REBEL EUROPE

REBEL EUROPE

How America Can Live with a Changing Continent

James Oliver Goldsborough

Macmillan Publishing Co., Inc.
NEW YORK

Collier Macmillan Publishers
LONDON

Macmillan Publishing Co., Inc.
866 Third Avenue, New York, N.Y. 10022
Collier Macmillan Canada, Inc.

Library of Congress Cataloging in Publication Data

Goldsborough, James Oliver.
    Rebel Europe.

    Includes bibliographical references and index.
        1. Europe—Relations—United States.
2. United States—Relations—Europe. 3. Europe—
Foreign relations—1945–   . 4. Europe—Economic
conditions—1945–   . 5. United States—Foreign
opinion, European. 6. Public opinion—Europe.
I. Title.
D1065.U5G64   327.4073   81-19285
ISBN 0-02-544570-7   AACR2

---

10   9   8   7   6   5   4   3   2   1

Printed in the United States of America

FOR ALEX AND KELLY

Contents

Preface

"There is nothing permanent except change."
HERACLITUS, 513 B.C.

THIS IS A BOOK about change, change in a particular place—Europe. It is not change that is irrelevant to Americans, for it affects us, both in its influence on us and in the ways it alters Europe's relationship to us. It is change that can be charted in Europe from north to south and east to west. It is not change that lies all in the same direction, if by direction is meant movement from left to right or right to left. Just as there is nothing consistent about the direction, there is nothing consistent about the causes, save the will to change. It is not a puritanical lust to return to conservative values nor revolutionary zeal for social experiment. In a sense it is change for change's sake. As in the French saying, *plus ça change, plus c'est la même chose,* it is a demonstration that in Europe, as elsewhere, change is the natural order of things, something we have tended to forget.

It is change in Poland and Hungary and change in France. It is change in Germany for over a decade. It is change in Britain, where the British had forgotten that capitalism is competition. It is change in Spain and Portugal, which had slumbered under faded dictatorships while the rest of Europe went modern. It is change in Greece, no longer a place of airy islets but the newest member of the European Community, which must learn to compete with German industry and French agriculture and to defend its exchange rate. It is change in the small countries of Benelux and Scandinavia, becoming vaguely pacifist as the threat of war in Europe is replaced by fears of lost Middle East oil supplies. It is change in Russia, caught in the cruelest of dilemmas, exposed to the crumbling of empire and the failure of doctrine and wondering if salvation lies in accepting the change, as it must someday, or putting it off again with one more retreat into autarky, militarism, interventionism.

This is an essay on what change is doing to Europe, East and West. The story goes back to de Gaulle, who first told us that the division of Europe that grew out of World War II was unnatural and could not endure. Once more, de Gaulle was ahead of his time. It is ironic that a decade after his death his place should be taken by a former archrival, Mitterrand, whose style and vision is as Gaullist as was de Gaulle's. De Gaulle died disillusioned, not discredited, and his ideas did not die at all. The policies pursued across Europe, East and West, almost from the time of his death in 1970 and throughout the decade of the 1970s were Gaullist. It was a decade dedicated to diminishing the gulf, bridging the gap, ending the division imposed on Europe by the political collapse of Germany.

If de Gaulle's disillusionment by 1968 had come to focus on Russia, Europe's disillusionment today is with America. While Americans have been looking the other way, riddled with the misfortunes and disasters that have hounded us since the 1960s, Europe quietly has moved away from us, in a direction de Gaulle could only approve. If postwar Europeans believed Europe need only to hitch its star to America, which, like Daedalus, builder of wings, would pull it through the cosmos to the promised land, their successors identify us more with Icarus, Daedalus' son who plunged from the sky. If good fortune is either to be right or be lucky, the United States has had a long run of misfortune. As we have reeled from one drama to another—Vietnam, assassinations, race riots, Watergate, crime, inflation, devaluation, energy penury, an arms race, weak Presidents—our friends in Europe have increasingly marked their distance, never too abruptly, never too publicly, always steadily.

As we have come to doubt our own motives and seek salvation

in simplistic formulas, the Europeans have gained confidence and shown ability to deal with complex interrelationships. As we have elected new and untried Presidents and failed spectacularly at reaching national consensus either on foreign or economic policy, the Europeans have gained ground. As we have vacillated between indecision and bluster, isolationism and militarism, narcissism and interventionism, ceasing to be a model for the world, they have stepped forward with new solutions, often taking from us roles we had played for a quarter century.

American foreign correspondents are in a unique position to observe foreign events. Unlike others who write about foreign affairs, they become, if they are true to their vocation, expatriates, immersing themselves in the new lands, burrowing into them like a weevil to describe it to Americans. Since newspaper correspondents write for the people as a whole rather than special segments of it, our reporting is broad, not limited to specialized themes, such as economics, business, or diplomacy. Today the story may be an interview with the President, but the following day it is with the President's *concierge*; today it is how the people work, tomorrow how they play, fight, love, eat.

The correspondents' advantage is that they spend a lifetime abroad. If not a lifetime, it is a good many years, in my case fifteen. It is a rich life, but it is one fraught with inconveniences, not the least of which is that you are away from home, and the longer you're away the more homesick you get. If you can put up with that, few jobs match it, for you are never bored. You are sustained by the simple knowledge that you are the main source of America's knowledge about the world, and in these inward-looking times that may matter.

Europe, the focus of this book, was home for most of my professional life. Having gone to Paris to work for the old Paris edition of the *New York Herald Tribune* in 1964, I stayed on until 1979. By the time I left I had reported from twenty-nine European countries, every one but four: San Marino, Malta, Albania, and Bulgaria. That span of time, a decade and a half, covered three separate phases in European-American relations: Phase I, which began after World War II, was our proconsul phase; Phase II, beginning in the 1960s, marked the period when the Europeans, individually and collectively, began to question their future as American colonies; Phase III, which began with the 1970s and is the main focus of this book, has been a period of both *bouleversement* and *renversement,* as the Europeans, taking advantage of our mistakes, gained control of many of the cards of power we formerly held. Not only have we seen our stake diminished as the game progressed, but in many ways it no longer is a friendly game. For a foreign observer, it helped, indeed was necessary, to be present during at least part of all three of the phases. To appreciate how things are today, one needs some memory of the Europe of the rubble, or at very least, *Europe on $5.00 a day.*

When the Carnegie Endowment decided some years back to commission returning foreign correspondents to do larger works based on whatever knowledge they might have gleaned abroad, it was with the idea of tapping new sources of foreign policy writing, sources with first-hand experience which might be useful in helping us to shape policy and pursue our national interests. One could argue that we have made a mistake in leaving the reporting of foreign affairs too much in the hands of academic "experts," men of great erudition but little experience. This is a failing that has become particularly important in the field of strategic studies. Expertise, *a priori,* implies a defect: to have become an expert at one thing means to have foregone other things. One is knowledgeable, not wise; educated, not worldly. Among experts today, we find few examples of the kind of polymath who lived a century or two ago and had the time and the leisure to become expert (and perhaps wise) in many fields.

If foreign policy experts are to be treated with caution, probably nothing imperils the world more than their strategic counterpart, the defense specialists with their Ph.D. treatise on the circular error probability of counterforce capability who emerge from a burrow from time to time in attempts to convince the public that their theoretical model is a description of the real world. These specialists wed themselves to politicians who become champions of billion-dollar weapons to close missile "gaps" and "windows of vulnera-bility." These people bear a prime responsibility for the arms race. They believe, as writer Roscoe Drummond has described it, in going "all out for strategic nuclear weapons; they are the glamour weapons and funding them hastily is attractive." The military-industrial complex, which President Eisenhower denounced as one of the major ills of our society twenty years ago, has today taken on the glamour of strategic technology. "Some day," Ike wrote to his friend Sweed Hazlett, "there is going to be a man sitting in my present chair who has not been raised in the military services and who will have little understanding of where slashes in their esti-mates can be made with little or no damage."

This is a book based on long foreign experience, considerable research by the large and competent staff of professionals and in-terns at Carnegie and, I hope, common sense. It tries to relate the loosening of the Atlantic relationship in a way that suggests the loosening is not only inevitable, but positive. Policies don't last forever. We have come a long way with the ones we have and today need to make adjustments for a world that has changed. We have changed as well, and are changing, as the succeeding semes-ters of young interns who come to Carnegie never fail to remind me. By and large, I will feel more confident when the running of affairs has been turned over to them.

REBEL EUROPE

CHAPTER 1

The Winds of Change

"The relationship between Western Europe and North America, alias the Atlantic Alliance, is in the early stages of what could be a terminal illness."

The *Economist*,
June 6, 1981

THERE HAS BEEN A TENDENCY in this country since the end of World War II to see Europe as a fixed continent, one doomed, forever, to the status quo. Defying all historical precedent, this view holds that the Europe that grew out of World War II and Hitler's defeat, and which matured during the cold war, has been defined for perpetuity, divided by Soviet and American fiat into eastern and western dependencies. The view is that so long as the American and Soviet "condominium" does not desire change in Europe, there will be none, for the eastern half is locked too tightly into Soviet control to do anything, whereas the western half is too divided and vulnerable to influence events.

The intellectual rationale for this unchanging Europe—which would become the first of the populated continents ever successfully to resist change—was laid out in a masterful little book which once was required reading in undergraduate political science courses, *The Political Collapse of Europe,* written by Hajo Holborn in 1951. Holborn's analysis had an immediate and mesmerizing effect on American foreign policy. He was describing and analyzing the political consequences of the destruction of Nazi Germany and of the unofficial spheres of influence agreement among Churchill, Roosevelt, and Stalin at Yalta in 1945. His conclusion was that the total collapse of Germany in the war had led to the permanent political collapse of Europe.

In World War II, which was decided by the participation of the Soviet Union and the United States, the collapse of the traditional European system became an irrevocable fact. What is commonly called the "historic Europe" is dead and beyond resurrection. It is doubtful to what extent this statement has become common knowledge.[1]

That it didn't become common knowledge didn't matter very much. It certainly was official knowledge that the old Europe was dead, and that fact became the basis of our policy. In 1951, in the depths of the cold war, it would have been difficult to defend another thesis. Poland, East Germany, and Czechoslovakia had been locked effectively into the Soviet sphere, isolating those nations from the West. Stalin still was exercising power ruthlessly, the world still two years from his death and five years from Khrushchev's de-Stalinization. Stalin had unleashed the North Koreans against South Korea, a gesture so incomprehensible that the West could only view it as a prelude to similar aggression in Europe.

No one seriously challenged Holborn's thesis during the 1950s. Every political event, no matter how unexpected or dramatic, seemed to confirm it: the rise of the military blocs; the suppression of revolts in East Germany, Poland, and Hungary; the repeated Soviet attempts to cut off West Berlin; all argued persuasively that the Soviet Union would permit no changes in its Eastern European empire. Even the change in mood that followed Stalin's death, the new Soviet leaders' message of "peaceful coexistence" and evident desire to put limits on the East-West rivalry of the previous decade, were interpreted as indications that the Russians considered the conquests of 1945 a *bien aquis* and therefore could adopt a less paranoid—though no less rigid—posture concerning their European empire.

On the Western side, events substantiated Holborn's thesis as well. The formation of the European Economic Community in 1957 demonstrated that continental Western Europe was abandoning hope of reconciliation with the East and turning attention to its own integration. Britain's choice to stay outside the Community and in close relationship with the Commonwealth and the United States suggested that Western Europe would remain divided and weak.

Following his return to power in 1958, President Charles de Gaulle's disapproval of the Community provided evidence that it would remain ineffective.

Over the years the Holborn thesis came to serve not only as explanation of the political collapse of Europe, but as explanation of its cultural and moral decline as well. In our time, as the political decline of the Continent came to be accepted as the normal and permanent state of affairs, we have tended to focus even more on the psychic aspects of Europe's political collapse. This has taken the form of a proliferation of writing on Europe's decline and decay. Beginning in 1950 with a book by L. B. Namier called *Europe in Decay* (at a time when Europe actually *was* in physical decay), the same basic thesis continues to be defended thirty years later. Taking a random sampling from the past few years, we find such works as *A Continent Astray*,[2] *Defense de l'Europe Decadent*,[3] *Atlantis Lost*,[4] *Europe Between the Superpowers*,[5] "Looking for Europe."[6] The titles vary, but the themes do not: Western Europe is experiencing what the sociologists call a climacteric, a biological term used to describe the life cycle; Europe is in a dead, or at least moribund phase. It is on the tail end of the life cycle, having more or less run its course, destined to have little to say about its own future, much less the world's.

These are updated and sophisticated versions of Holborn. Holborn argued that the Soviet-American hegemony had led to the "breakdown of Europe as a political system, balanced within itself." Now we are told that the political breakdown has led to all sorts of morbid psychic symptoms. We have entered Gramsci's "interregnum," when the old is dying and the new still unborn. Western Europe is in a state of "abulia," defined as a "paralysis of will" in which you may want to act, but are unable to. The Continent has been rendered a pitiful, helpless ex-giant through its inability to defend itself or solve its social, economic, and political problems.

Just as Turkey a century ago was the "sick man of Europe," today there are several candidates for the bed (though few would admit that Turkey has vacated it). If, a century ago, we had a single disease, today it is an epidemic. There are treatises on the "English disease" (which, two centuries ago, was the Continental name for syphilis), the "French disease," (the English name for the same malady), the "Italian disease," "Dutch disease," and so on. Collectively, these diseases offer the patient no hope for recovery. Thus, we are told in a description that certainly does no mincing: "that Europe today is in a state of decline cannot be seriously disputed."[7] Or again, Europe is characterized by "narcissism, abdication and retreat from concern for power on the world stage."[8]

The trouble with this view of a stagnant and decadent Europe is not just that it is irrelevantly dated. The trouble is that it is misleading and pernicious for America. Since our perceptions and policies are based on outmoded and egocentric views, we are continually being surprised by European actions, East and West, that are not consistent with our view of what they should be. We persist in trying to force the Europeans back into our mold, when what we need is a new mold.

Our difficulties with Western Europe have become to a large degree psychic ones. They did not exist during the cold war, because Europe was in a state of near-total political and economic dependency and unable to act. Lacking freedom of action, its policies could have no moral quality. Put in Sartrian terms, Europe's lack of choice and alternative meant it could have no responsibility. Most of us grew up knowing a Western Europe that was indeed the perfect ally: too weak to disagree, yet not so weak as to be totally irrelevant for us. The relationship between us is different today, but we have failed to perceive how different it is.

With a prosperity in some cases surpassing ours and a culture and quality of life in many ways superior, Europe today chafes under the old relationship. There has been a drifting apart within the Atlantic Alliance, one that is only partially checked during times of East-West crisis. It was not so long ago that international crisis brought near total solidarity among members of the Alliance. Even the French, at best reluctant allies, would drift back to the fold during difficult periods—during the Cuban crisis of 1962, for example, and again in 1968 when Czechoslovakia was invaded. The Afghanistan and Polish crises, however, have demonstrated how international crisis today is insufficient to create an identity of Atlantic views.

Hajo Holborn argued that so long as Russians and Americans opposed change in Europe there was nothing the Europeans could do about it. For more than a decade after he wrote, this was true. We had not only the quite obvious fact that Eastern Europe was locked into the Soviet orbit, but that Western Europe, balkanized and rent by historical and ethnic rivalry, was unable either to unify itself or to improve its relations with the East. In trying to do both, it succeeded in doing neither.

What did the future hold for this once mighty Continent, birthplace of Western culture, philosophy, and science; of the Renaissance and the Enlightenment? Politically dependent, culturally dead, morally decadent, scientifically stagnant, Europe seemed finished. In France, in 1967, a little book was published that seemed to tie up all these unfortunate ends. Called *Le Défi Americain* (The American Challenge), it offered little hope. It seemed to confirm Holborn and Europe's climacteric. The New World, to paraphrase Canning, had not been called into existence to redress the balance of the Old but to take its place.

The flaw in the Holborn analysis was to postulate a permanent condition from a temporary arrangement. This has been done before in Europe. No matter how compelling may be the "Myth of Yalta"—which holds that Roosevelt, Churchill, and Stalin divided Europe permanently into Eastern and Western halves at the Yalta Conference in 1945—why should it have more claim to permanence than countless similar arrangements whose names and dates litter the history books? What gave Holborn its compelling quality was the central idea: that 1945 represented a watershed, that all future history would be different because Europe no longer was internally coherent, but had fallen, both parts of it, under external control. Europe's destiny, unlike in the past, was no longer in European hands, but in those of Americans and Russians. The corner-stone of the thesis, the central arch on which the whole structure rested, was that Russians and Americans would prevent change. One sees the problem. On the one hand, the American hegemony is maintained by consent, not force. If Western Europe wants to end the arrangement for whatever reasons, we can oppose it by any manner of diplomatic, economic, and political means; it is unlikely we will go to war. The Soviet Union, on the other hand, while keeping its European half in line through power, is itself a Euro-pean nation (at least partially so) and thus under the influence of the other Europeans. The Soviet Union, as time passes, perceives it has other pressing problems—in Asia, with its own economy, with its minorities—and this increases the leverage of the Europe-ans, East and West alike. The Poles, in particular, were eager to test the new margins of maneuver. If the Russians hesitated to stop them, it was because Moscow understood the risks involved. What would Soviet Communism gain in a war against Polish workers?

In the West two historical figures would challenge Holborn. Charles de Gaulle, returning to power in France in 1958 after twelve years in the political desert, spent his first term ending the war in Algeria, preventing civil war, and creating the institutions of the Fifth Republic. By 1965 and his second term he was ready to turn to the world. Though lacking means (when did de Gaulle *have* the means?), he used France's limited power with consum-mate skill. The crux of de Gaulle's argument was the United States and Soviet Union were not equal superpowers; the United States was far stronger, and, from the French view, American economic domination was as dangerous as a hypothetical Soviet military threat. The Soviet Union, de Gaulle said in 1966, would not attack Western Europe.[9] It was time for more reasonable relations with Moscow. The United States was trying to rule Europe and wage a dangerous war in Southeast Asia simultaneously. It was time for Western Europe to take its distance. France was beginning to do so. "American hegemony, dependence on the United States, is a bad policy for France," he said. "It inhibits faith in self and inhibits others from faith in the countries of Europe. It has to be realized that France exists, and Germany and Britain."[10]

De Gaulle withdrew French forces from NATO and removed NATO headquarters from France. In June 1965 he became the first Western leader to visit Russia since the cold war, a symbolic trip on which he first talked of a "Europe of Europeans." At one point he told the Russians, "I am very pleased the existence of the Soviet Union should cancel out the danger of American hegemony just as I am pleased the United States should be there to cancel out the danger of Soviet hegemony."[11] Three months later, before 100,000 Cambodians and Prince Norodom Sihanouk in Phnom-Penh, de Gaulle made his strongest anti-Vietnam war speech, speaking of a "war condemned by numerous peoples of Europe, Africa and Latin America, and, ultimately, more and more threatening to the peace of the world."[12]

The Russians were, obviously, delighted by these policies. In de Gaulle's anti-Americanism they saw a means of weakening NATO and the American influence in Europe—precisely de Gaulle's stated policy. But the Soviets, aware of France's limited power, were more guarded in their policy toward France than de Gaulle would have liked. They did not spurn him, for they felt his influence on West Germany. But a Franco-Russian relationship that was too spectacular would have pushed Bonn even more snugly into the American embrace, a development that, since Ludwig Erhard replaced Konrad Adenauer in 1964, was already underway.

The first Western leader with the will and the vision to alter the status quo in Europe, de Gaulle saw his schemes crash on the plains of Slovakia. The Soviet invasion of Czechoslovakia in August 1968 was a profound shock to him. Though one of his chief lieutenants, Michel Debré, would refer to Czechoslovakia as an *accident de parcours* (routine accident), anybody in Paris that terrible spring (for two months, in May and June, Paris had been the scene of the student and worker strikes and riots) knew how de Gaulle took it. Prague was a crushing blow to his view of a Europe from the At-

7

lantic to the Urals. No one felt the Russians were coming westward. But the time of a "Europe for the Europeans" was not yet ripe. De Gaulle was ahead of his time.

Seven months after Prague, de Gaulle left power, victim of an irrelevant political vote on decentralization of power. His departure coincided with the arrival of Willy Brandt as chancellor of West Germany, the first Social Democrat to hold that post since the Weimar Republic. Judging from most accounts, de Gaulle and Brandt had gotten along well. De Gaulle may have seen the political greatness hiding in Brandt's hulking frame. Certainly the two had little in common personally: de Gaulle, rigid, self-assured, conservative; Brandt, insecure, moody, a *Norddeutscher,* (the term Germans use for people from the Baltic—distant, brooding, introspective types).

Brandt, like de Gaulle, had a vision, and it was this common vision of Europe that drew the two men together. Said de Gaulle to Brandt:

France is in no way opposed to America. On the contrary, she is America's friend. But nothing can be worse for the Europeans than an American hegemony which enfeebles Europe and prevents the Europeans from being themselves. Such hegemony also hinders agreement with the East—in fact, it hinders everything. The Americans are Americans, not Europeans.[13]

Such remarks, writes Brandt, evoked the following feeling in him: "Why only he? The Federal Republic must not create the impression it had no will or interest of its own. . . . Why only he?"[14]

Brandt came to power a year after Prague and made it clear he planned to pick up where de Gaulle left off. His timing was right. The invasion of Czechoslovakia had been a disaster for Soviet prestige in Europe and the world, and Moscow was searching for new initiatives. Prague had set back East-West relations but not broken them. The Nixon Administration had been in office for eight months when Brandt was elected, and the first SALT talks were about to begin. In March, 1969, at a Warsaw Pact conference in Bucharest, Moscow relaunched its proposal for a conference on security and cooperation in Europe—an idea that had been gaining ground prior to Prague, but which was shelved afterward. Preparations for NATO–Warsaw Pact talks on mutual force reductions were about to begin. It was in this atmosphere that Brandt revealed the outlines of his *Ostpolitik*, his plans for West Germany's reconciliation with the East.

That reconciliation had cautiously begun in 1966 with the election of a coalition of Christian Democrats and Social Democrats. But it took the new Brandt government, elected in 1969, to go all the way—accept the guilt that was still Germany's in the eyes of East Europe, accept the Oder-Neisse frontier between Poland and East Germany as permanent, and recognize the division of Germany. In a line that would become famous, Brandt said, "To change the status quo, we must first accept it."

Events tumbled quickly ahead after 1969. Bonn signed treaties with Prague, Warsaw, East Germany, and Moscow. A four-power Berlin treaty was signed in which Moscow recognized the legal link between West Berlin and West Germany. The change in West German policy under Brandt eventually would make possible the long-discussed European security conference, the idea that had been steadily building steam and which eventually was supported by every nation in Europe, East and West. It is one of the symbolic ironies of our times that—even when every continental European member of the Atlantic Alliance had rallied to support the Helsinki negotiations—the United States still hesitated. We went to Helsinki, but as followers, not leaders. And we were surprised at its outcome, which East and West Europeans alike believe was more favorable to them than to the Soviet Union.

We have been overconditioned by the Holborn thesis. We have been overinfluenced by our closest European allies, the British, who, like us, are uncomfortable with change. Is it part of an Anglo-Saxon aging process to grow conservative? Is it that our two nations, having developed their own immutable political institutions, think every other nation has reached a similar point of immobility? What we must face today is the evidence that Europe is no more resistant to change than any other continent. As Professor Lawrence T. Caldwell has written: "The hegemony these two powers (the

United States and the Soviet Union) exercised over their respective alliances (has) eroded dramatically.''[15] We may become the last to discover this, even after the Soviet Union, which surely understands that the margin for maneuver of the Eastern Europeans is increasing the same as that of the Western Europeans. Can Moscow launch an invasion each time to block the changes, to thwart each new protest movement? Such policy would be no policy at all. As Talleyrand remarked on Napoleon's failures: "You can do everything with bayonets except sit on them."

As for Western Europe, it has today come back from the abyss, culturally, morally, and politically. "No one can doubt," wrote Raymond Aron, "that France changed more in the quarter century between 1948 and 1973 than in the whole of the previous century."[16] The changes in the 1980s already show signs of being just as great, and the same is true for West Germany. It seemed difficult to believe that these changes would not lead to new courses of action in foreign policy. The Franco-German relationship today is solid. However slowly and reluctantly, Britain is becoming daily more European, less Atlantic and Commonwealth-oriented (39 percent of British trade today is with the EEC, compared with 18 percent when Britain joined in 1974). In coming years, Western Europe will become a more cohesive political force able to assume more world responsibility.

Is this in America's interest? Is this something we should support, oppose, or, lacking the decisiveness to do either, simply stand back and make sure we do nothing to encourage? For a quarter century we have avoided giving a firm answer to the question. Since the founding of the EEC in 1957 we have maintained a double policy that has consisted of saying one thing and doing another. We have professed to believe in European unity, but our policies have sought to undermine it. Such attitudes were once comprehensible. Why aid a process of emancipation from us? For a quarter century we have declined to contribute to a process designed to diminish our influence in Europe and have seen our influence diminished to a greater degree than had we directed the process ourselves.

Above all, it has cost us money. As a new American Administration came into office with grandiose plans for building a wartime defense industry without raising taxes to pay for it (indeed, with tax decreases), the Europeans looked on bemused. They did not complain, for better the United States spending more on defense than Europe, they thought. At the Ottawa economic summit meeting in mid-1981 they asked President Reagan the following question: Did he understand that an American policy of budget deficits and high interest rates would force European interest rates so high that the Europeans would be forced to trim their budgets and reduce defense spending, exacerbating Alliance tensions? They received no answer. The result: West Germany soon announced it could not fully meet a planned 3 percent defense increase and eliminated some new weapons projects; Britain began cutting back its Navy. There was an old law at work here: when the United States spends more for defense, Europe spends less. Collective military buildups in the Alliance have been notorious failures.

But it was just as clear the Europeans did not agree with the new Administration policy of all arms buildup and no arms control. For Europe, these things go together. They have never forgiven us for the failure to ratify the Salt II treaty, a failure the *Times* (London) called a prime factor in "undermining Europe's confidence" in America.[17] For Europe, SALT II had been a first step toward SALT III, aimed at cutting back on Soviet missiles directed at Europe itself.

The real danger of the new American policy was that it would accelerate what one European commentator called the widening gap between Europeans and Americans on the Soviet Union.[18] Europe, whose policy toward Moscow became more complex during the final year of the Carter Administration, under Reagan took on the role of intermediary between the superpowers. Hardly had the new Administration settled into office than a host of European statesmen stopped by Blair House to give advice to the new President. Their visits were preludes to similar visits to Moscow. At least they still came to Washington first.

Though Reagan got off to a better start with his visitors than had

Carter, it was not by much. The Europeans didn't like shelving arms control, didn't understand the hoopla over El Salvador, questioned the Administration's intentions toward South Africa and the Middle East, doubted Reaganomics, questioned a military policy based on new nuclear weapons such as the neutron bomb and medium-range missiles but without conscription, and wondered about a policy of anti-Communist containment that probably spelled more trouble for the Alliance than it did for the Russians.

Beyond these policy differences, there was a deeper level of philosophical difference that was driving Europeans and Americans apart. Europe did not understand our predilection to view all the world through military and superpower prisms. Not only did Europeans believe this was wrong, but they found it self-defeating, for it left out of the equation the true strengths of America. Perhaps nobody put the perplexity better than West German political scientist Uwe Nerlich:

The new American preoccupation with military superiority—alien to American political traditions—has been a major factor in the decline of American values and institutions over the last two decades, a process that has served the purposes of Soviet diplomacy well.[19]

Notes for Chapter 1

1. Hajo Holborn, *The Political Collapse of Europe* (New York: Knopf, 1951), p. xi.

2. Walter Laqueur, *A Continent Astray* (New York: Oxford University Press, 1977).

3. Raymond Aron, *Defense de l'Europe Decadent* (Paris: Robert Laffont, 1977).

4. James Chace and Earl Ravenal, Eds., *Atlantis Lost* (New York: Council of Foreign Relations, 1975).

5. Anton DePorte, *Europe between the Superpowers* (New Haven: Yale University Press, 1979).

6. ———, "Looking for Europe," *Daedalus* 107 (Winter 1979).

7. Laqueur, *A Continent Astray*, p. 4.

8. Stanley Hoffmann, *Primacy or World Order*, (New York: McGraw-Hill, 1978), p. 64.

9. Quoted in Willy Brandt, *People and Politics* (Boston: Little, Brown, 1979), p. 131.

10. *Ibid.*, p. 132.

11. Alexander Werth, *De Gaulle*, (Middlesex, UK: Penguin Books, 1965), p. 407.

12. *Ibid.*, p. 412.

13. Brandt, *People and Politics*, p. 132.

14. Brandt, *People and Politics*, p. 123.

15. Lawrence T. Caldwell, "The Future of Soviet-American Relations," *Soviet-American Relations in the 1980s*, Council of Foreign Relations, New York, 1980, p. 24.

16. Aron, *Defense de l'Europe Decadent*, p. 213.

17. *Times* (London), March 3, 1981, p. 13.

18. Joseph Joffe, "European-American Relations: The Enduring Crisis," *Foreign Affairs*, Spring 1981, p. 845.

19. Uwe Nerlich, "Change in Europe: A Secular Trend?" *Daedalus*, Winter 1981, p. 86.

CHAPTER 2

The Euro-Atlantic Triangle

"In spite of its wealth, in spite (or because) of its culture and its free-
doms, Western Europe as a whole does not think it is capable of defending itself without assistance."[1]

RAYMOND ARON

THIS NOTION of a group of prosperous nations (which now exceeds
the United States in gross national product) being unwilling to do
what is necessary to defend itself is what most American critics
mean today when they refer to Europe's "decadence." It is also
the subject of Raymond Aron's analysis in his *Defense de l'Europe
Decadent*. What, asks Aron, if the rest of this century and all of
the next belong to "the producers, and not to the warriors?"[2]

If a nation's decadence is defined as its inability to defend itself
without outside help, then the countries of Europe have been decadent for more than a century. Unlike the United States, few have
been willing to stand alone in the face of potential aggression, and
most have sought assistance in the form of alliance. That the assistance came from within or without Holborn's "European system"
seems irrelevant. Nineteenth century Europe was one of shifting
international alliances designed to create equilibrium, the deterrent
of past centuries. As another historian has noted:

At the end of the nineteenth century all the great powers except Great
Britain were involved in formal alliances; and in the twentieth century
Great Britain and even the United States have been drawn into the compli-
cated structure of guarantees and pacts of mutual assistance.[3]

Let us agree, then, that such a definition of decadence does not
mean much. The United States, more isolated, needs alliances less,
even today. If Britain, France, or West Germany seeks alliance

with the United States today, in other times they have sought it with each other or with the Soviet Union or even Japan. In today's world of two superpowers, each with massively expensive strategic nuclear forces, it must seem reasonable to smaller nations to have one of the superpowers as an ally so long as the other is perceived as a threat or so long as they are too weak to end the alliance. In the first case it is cheaper than building up their own deterrents, and in the second it is accepting the inevitable.

The equation changes, however, in several cases. It changes the moment you start losing faith in your superpower. It may come to be perceived as significantly enough weakened to be vulnerable either to the other superpower or to you. Instead of fundamental equilibrium existing, with stalemate, a more dynamic situation prevails, allowing for change. In the case of the Eastern Europeans, locked into involuntary alliance with the Soviet Union, the stalemate was challenged in the 1950s and 1960s by local leaders overestimating Moscow's vulnerability and underestimating Russian willingness to use military strength to resist change. Today it is Poland's turn to challenge, and this time the timing may be right.

A similar dynamic is at work in Western Europe, where it is widely believed today that the United States cannot be counted on to risk a strategic nuclear war to defend European interests. This is not to say we would not use our armed forces stationed in Europe if Europe is attacked. It simply means we would not risk confrontation with the Soviets to defend *all* European interests. Brandt makes the point in his memoirs, writing about the Berlin Wall:

We lost certain illusions . . . [East German leader Walter] Ulbricht had been allowed to take a swipe at the western superpower and the United States had merely winced with annoyance. . . . my political deliberations in the years that followed were substantially influenced by the day's [August 13, 1961] experience, and it was against this background that my so-called Ostpolitik—the beginning of détente—took shape. . . . My new and inescapable realization was that traditional patterns of western policy had proved ineffective, if not downright unrealistic.[4]

Just as the relationship with an allied superpower loses importance if the superpower is perceived to be losing strength, so, too, is it weakened if the hostile superpower is perceived as less of a threat. In Atlantic relations since the 1960s this perception has played a stronger role than any notion of our fading strength. This is a key point. The difficulties dominating Atlantic affairs are not caused by any European feeling that America is less resolved today to help Europe defend itself against outside attack than it once was. The difficulties exist because relations between Eastern and Western Europe have improved. Détente has created a different relationship between the United States and Soviet Union from that between Western Europe and the Soviet Union. It therefore has altered the Atlantic relationship as well.

Détente, as Henry Kissinger recognized, always represented a threat to the alliance. It was no accident that President Nixon and Kissinger resisted *Ostpolitik,* the improvement of relations between West Germany and Eastern Europe. Kissinger recounts a visit by Brandt to Nixon in Key Biscayne in late 1971.

Brandt thought that the Soviets genuinely wished détente partly because of their fear of China. He expressed his gratification at NATO's support for his Ostpolitik. Nixon frostily corrected him, saying that the Alliance did not *object* to the policy.[5]

Few citations better illustrate the divergence that was taking place. For Nixon and Kissinger the NATO alliance had become a policy *end.* Détente was judged to the degree that it served that policy end—preservation of the alliance. But for the Europeans, the alliance was a *means,* something born to respond to a cold war situation and expendable once that situation changed—once they had achieved what one European commentator called, "a deep-seated sense of security born out of thirty-five years of peace gelling into ultrastability."[6]

The Soviet invasion of Afghanistan was a demonstration of the third case in which an ally may want to distance itself from a superpower: when the allied relationship appears not so much a source of security as one of danger. If the superpowers are indeed on a collision course, it may be best to keep one's distance.

16

The Western Europeans did not react to Afganistan as we did, and instead took the view that the Soviet invasion was a strategic error that in the long term could only undermine Soviet influence in the Moslem and Third World countries in addition to putting a severe strain on Soviet resources. Brandt's successor, Helmut Schmidt, stated the difference in Atlantic views:

If the United States deems it necessary to apply measures against the Soviet Union, it can count on the support of the Federal Republic of Germany as a completely reliable ally and friend. But . . . we will not permit what we have achieved in ten years of defense and détente policy to be disparaged or torn down.[7]

West Germany, in other words, would not take the same measures. Wrote Rudolf Augstein, publisher of *Der Spiegel*, in an editorial entitled "Détente is Divisible": "Détente is not something we can give up for anybody."[8]

Gaullism is rampant in Europe today, rampant to the point that we must ask ourselves if a new triangle has not arisen to take its place next to the strategic triangle (USSR, China, United States) and trilateralism (United States, Japan, Europe). The new triangle, which can be called the Euro-Atlantic triangle, has taken the place of what was the simpler bilateral East-West relationship. The significance of Afghanistan to Atlantic relations is not that it created anything, but that, like photographic processing, it brought out impressions that had been latent.

As we have seen, Atlantic relations had been evolving for more than a decade. If Afghanistan added anything to the equation, it was that for the first time Atlantic differences were not over military strategy, energy, or economics but over what was the very centerpiece of the alliance itself: the Soviet Union. The process of détente in Europe during the 1970s had created a fundamental Atlantic divergence. Prior to Afghanistan, during the high water of détente, United States–Soviet relations on one hand and Euro-Soviet relations on the other had seemed to be improving symmetrically. Détente may have taken different forms in Europe and America, but the essence appeared the same. Today we see how different it really was.

For Europe, an organic East-West political and economic relationship has begun to install itself, accompanied, to be sure, by doubts and suspicion on both sides, but real nonetheless. American critics of European attitudes argue that the Europeans are being tricked, Finlandized, neutralized, allowing themselves to be drawn into a relationship in which Europe needs the Soviet Union more than the Soviet Union needs Europe. But not everybody agrees. One study concluded: "By and large the Soviet leadership needs, or thinks it needs, this (economic) cooperation more than we need or think we need it."[9] The leverage was ours, not theirs. Eastern Europe's growing dependence on the West became painfully apparent during the Polish crisis. Poland, with $25 billion in Western debts and servicing payments of $7 billion per year, turned desperately in every direction for funds to keep its economy going. At one point, when the Poles were bankrupt, the Soviet Union was paying Warsaw's debt to the West. Wrote Italian commentator Arrigo Levi: "It can be claimed that without détente the 'new Poland' of Gdansk workers would not have come into existence."[10]

Détente has meant less to the United States both economically and politically than to Europe. Indeed, as Stanley Hoffmann has suggested, it may be that Americans never have correctly understood détente, that both Nixon and Kissinger were guilty of having "oversold détente" and of convincing us that we had forged iron levers that could perpetually influence Soviet policy when we had not.[11] This would explain why, with each new Soviet transgression—whether Angola, Ethiopia, Afghanistan or El Salvador—we are ready to tear up the treaties, boycott the Russians, engage in a new arms race.

The Europeans, East and West, see détente differently. Soviet party leader Brezhnev has stated what détente is for Moscow:

Détente does not in the slightest abolish the laws of class struggle. Some bourgeois leaders affect surprise over the solidarity of Soviet Communists, the Soviet people, with the struggle of other peoples for freedom and progress. This is either outright naiveness or, more likely, a deliberate befuddling of minds. We make no secret of the fact that we see détente as the way to create more favorable conditions for peaceful socialist and Communist construction.[12]

The struggle in the Third World—in other words, the struggle for minds—goes on. As we shall see, it is a struggle the Russians are losing, not winning. Détente for Moscow, above all, is making sure this struggle does not escalate into war with the United States by impinging on United States interests. But there are gray areas. Our differences over Afghanistan came because Moscow did not see Afghanistan as a United States interest, while we tended to see it as bringing the Soviets so close to our Gulf oil interests that it became grounds for confrontation.

The Western European view of détente is that it primarily involves Europe. A former French Foreign Minister, Jean François-Ponçet, has defined détente as "designed essentially to heal the great wound of World War II, reconstitute the tissue of torn Europe in a quasi-biological sense."[13] This is not something the Europeans are willing to abandon to protest Soviet activities in Afghanistan any more than they were willing to renounce treaties and agreements with us to protest American activities in Vietnam. It follows, however, that a Soviet attack on Poland would be a different matter, would reopen the wounds healed by détente, destroy the agreement reached at Helsinki in which the European states renounced force as a means of settling disputes. A Soviet invasion of Poland would have incalculable results, leading not only to a disintegration of East-West relations but very probably to the disintegration of the Soviet East European empire as well. It was for this reason that Soviet commentators repeatedly referred to the Polish events as a "trap," one in which the Soviets were ensnared no matter what course of action they followed.

For many Americans détente is a Soviet trick, a sham, a smokescreen behind which Moscow can maneuver to bring down Western defenses and weaken the alliance. As sovietologist Dimitri Simes has put it, "There is no strong American constituency committed to improved relations with the Soviet Union."[14] There are many constituencies aligned against it. Even during the best days of détente—1974–1976—and Helsinki, Vladivostok, and the grain agreement, détente in America never seemed more than a necessary evil—*Realpolitik*. Even then, people did not like it. Ronald Reagan, in the 1976 Presidential campaign, forced President Ford to jettison the word; Jimmy Carter, running for President, claimed he would not have gone to Helsinki to sign the accord with the Europeans.

If there is no significant American constituency for détente with the Soviet Union, there is a large détente constituency in Western Europe. In France the political left is, expectedly, for good relations with Moscow (though in varying degrees), and the Gaullist right claims paternity of détente. In West Germany one might expect Soviet saber-rattling to strengthen the Christian-Democratic right at the expense of the Social Democrats. The fact is that each Soviet-inspired crisis has led to an increase in the Social Democratic Party's (SDP) vote. In September 1961, one month after the Berlin Wall was erected, the SDP made its first big breakthrough, climbing from 31.8 percent of the vote to 36.3 percent, its best performance since 1919. In the 1969 elections, one year after the Soviet invasion of Prague, the Social Democrats came to power for the first time since the war. It would seem that West German voters reason that with the SDP they can have both détente with the Soviet Union and defense by the United States, whereas with the Christian Democrats they can have only the latter.

The situations in the other Western European nations are somewhat different from those of France and West Germany. Britain, like us, never has had much sympathy for the Russians. Italy's policy on superpower questions is to adopt as low a profile as possible. It is the close identity of French and West German views on détente and the influence of these two most important Western European nations on the others that make it possible to talk loosely of a "Western European" view and of a Euro-Atlantic triangle.

While we have been trading grain and negotiating SALT with the Russians (both processes in limbo today), an organic economic relationship has grown up between Eastern and Western Europe. The Western Europeans believe that trade expansion into Eastern Europe is one of the great untapped economic resources of this century. The American view of Eastern European economic possibilities, however, is so limited that on a questionnaire mailed out to members of one prominent foreign policy association in 1980, Eastern Europe and the Soviet Union were not even included in a list of prime areas for business expansion (mentioned were Western Europe, the Middle East, Latin America, Asia, and Africa). United States business leaders would not agree. In hearings before a Congressional committee in 1978, American businessmen connected with Soviet trade made clear their view that the potential was great and that if we did not exploit it, the West Europeans and Japanese would. William Verity, president of Armco Corporation, gave Congress a list of twenty-eight major projects that the Soviets were letting to overseas concerns and projected the effect on the American economy of those projects.[15]

As things turned out, twenty-six of the twenty-eight projects were awarded by the Soviets to European or Japanese firms. American companies won two of them, a $353 million steel plant for Armco and a $100 million aluminum plant for Alcoa, both cancelled by the United States government following the invasion of Afghanistan. The Europeans and Japanese cancelled no contracts after Afghanistan, which added to the strains between Washington and the allies. What's more, though the Europeans (and Japanese) had promised not to take over any of the embargoed United States trade with Moscow, in reality they did. The French Creusot Loire steel group negotiated a $300 million steel mill at Novolipetsk, near Moscow, that looked strangely similar to the cancelled Armco plant, and West Germany's Klockner-Werke agreed to build a $311 million aluminum plant in Siberia in place of the Alcoa one. It looked more and more that the Europeans' idea of a "division of labor" was that Americans did the fighting and Europeans did the trading.

The Japanese, Italians, French, and Germans all held high-level trade talks with the Russians within weeks of the Afghanistan invasion. Even the loyal British showed signs of wanting to increase not decrease trade with Eastern Europe. In 1981 a Western European consortium led by the West Germans signed the biggest trade agreement in history with Moscow, a $4 billion first stage of an $11.8 billion deal to bring Siberian natural gas to Western Europe.

Table 1 shows that not only does EEC-USSR trade dwarf United States-USSR trade, but that it is basically balanced, whereas ours is not. What's more, the EEC-USSR trade is of a different nature.

TABLE 1

United States and Europe Community Trade with the Soviet Union

(in millions of dollars)

	1977	1978	1979	1980
United States				
exports to U.S.S.R.	1,627	2,252	3,607	941.0
imports from U.S.S.R.	235	540	874	544.0
European Community				
exports to U.S.S.R.	6,686	7,174	8,652	10,873.0
imports from U.S.S.R.	6,982	8,064	11,464	13,421.0

Source: OECD, *Statistics of Foreign Trade* (Series A, July 1980)

By 1979 both France and West Germany were importing over 3 percent of their oil from the Soviet Union. Bonn was importing 14 percent of its natural gas from the Soviet Union. The new natural gas agreement, when completed, would increase Soviet supply to 30 percent of German natural gas consumption by 1984. For Moscow exports of petroleum products to Western Europe had become the major source of Soviet hard currency. By 1979 Moscow was the largest supplier of enriched uranium to France and West Germany (a situation that developed following the Carter Administration's decision in 1977 to suspend United States deliveries of enriched uranium to France over disapproval of European nuclear policies). By 1980 West Germany had become the largest Western trade partner of every country in Eastern Europe.

There is no escaping that for many Americans this is decadent behavior, that there is something fundamentally abject about a group of nations (Western Europe) that profits from an economic relationship with a nation (the Soviet Union) while allowing another nation (the United States) to protect it from that nation. Few would deny that there is inconsistency of behavior in such policy. Until the last decade or so, the inconsistency did not appear quite so flagrant, because the prosperity and well-being of the profiting group did not appear quite so great. Moreover, American protection was a relatively simple affair since agreement between protector and protectorate was not difficult, and relations with the adversary were bad.

The situation has changed today. A growing number of Western Europeans also are unhappy with developments. No one calls for a break—and indeed no one wants one—but there is a feeling that what is needed is a redefinition of Atlantic relations, replacing dependency with autonomy. The absence of such a move has led to frequent recrimination and constant misunderstanding.

As one West German has put it:

For the United States, this means, above all, accepting the established political cooperation between European Economic Community members as a dominant West European policymaking process. If there is to be any coherence among West European policies, it will come primarily through this channel. There is no way for the political centrality of NATO to be reestablished. [16]

As we have seen, this urge toward autonomy in Western Europe has occasionally been confused in this country both with our own decline and with Europe's Finlandization. The view is wrong on both counts. It ignores that the European move away from us begun by de Gaulle was motivated not by too little United States power but by too much, and it confuses diffusion of power, which has been the dominant feature of the 1970s, with decline. Diffusion may be the opposite of decline. Decline may come from the attempt to block diffusion, as it did during Vietnam and is during Afghanistan.

That there has been a *relative* decline in United States power over the previous decade is generally accepted today, just as it is accepted there has been a decline in the relative power of all the countries of the industrialized world—including the Soviet Union. But the diminished American power has not gone to Moscow, faced with its own political and ideological defections. The gain in power has gone to the oil producers, to the nonaligned nations with their new political cartels, to fundamentalist Moslems, to the emerging giants of China, India, Indonesia. Some of it as well is going to the Western Europeans. The question for us is—is this pursuit of self-interest by our principal allies in conflict with our own self-interest when it is conceded that a considerable part of our "decline" relative to them was caused by the very burden of supporting and sustaining them?

As William Pfaff has written:

It would be a radical but liberating thought to consider that less might be more, and that what the United States and Western Europe need today is not closer alliance, restored alliance, or improved alliance, but less alliance. If less were to be expected of the relationship between the United States and the European states, the result—a more austere cooperation— might prove better adapted to what jointly we really need, and so there might be less abrasion and hypocrisy. In important respects, the present alliance is an anachronism.[17]

As for the charge of Europe's gradual Finlandization, a charge made most consistently by a hard-core, right-wing fringe of American opinion that simply does not bother to analyze the motivation behind European policy, the question arises that if Finlandization is taking place, who is Finlandizing whom? If Finlandization means anything, it means a nation subordinating its interests or values to accommodation with another. If that is the correct definition, Eastern Europe is being Finlandized as much as Western Europe. What do the recent events in Poland signify if not that Warsaw in recent years has been increasingly drawn out of the Communist system into a web of Western and world interdependencies? The more proper response is that Finlandization means nothing. The development of relations between Eastern and Western Europe during the past decade was not so much one region trying to dominate the other as the natural growth of economic and political relations between two halves of the same continent separated artificially by the cold war and striving to overcome the separation.

It is not only a diverging view of the Soviet Union that separates us. In general, the European view of America today is that of a nation whose problems are pressing. Their view of what is called *le Mal Americain* (the American disease) has little to do with what Americans see as the cause of our present troubles—namely, the Soviet Union. We are like two doctors reaching not only different but contradictory diagnoses. Americans see the Soviet Union as the root of all evil. The Europeans see America's problems as caused not by Russians but by Americans. The Europeans also deny that they are cringing in Finlandized fear before the Russians and tend to think, as Briton Michael Howard has put it, that "we are not more frightened of them than Americans, but rather less. I think we find it easier to see them as real people, with real, and alarming, problems of their own." [18] The United States is seen as ignoring the shift of power that took place in the 1970s, still living as it did in the 1950s, still believing that political and military solutions can be found for social and economic problems, confusing yesterday's East-West struggle with today's North-South one, still consuming 50 percent of the world's gasoline with 5 percent of the population.

We are seen as having deep-seated institutional problems, with a two-centuries-old outdated constitution that was, as Briton Robert Jackson has written, "designed for a society without strong governmental capabilities or ambitions," [19] and an inefficient system of separation of powers, as Bagehot said a century ago, designed on the principle of "having many sovereign authorities and hoping that their multitude may atone for their inferiority." On top of this, following the scandals of Watergate, we have taken to electing provincial Presidents lacking knowledge and experience not only of the world but of Washington. We are seen as having governments that do not understand the interaction between America's domestic and foreign policies, that believe we can scrap a seven-years-in-the-making SALT treaty without losing credibility and run 20 percent interest rates without suffering serious erosion in international influence.

No one, friend or foe, denies the resilience and power of the United States. But there should be little doubt that we are seen today as poorly inspired and poorly led. Europeans, like Americans, argue over the causes of the American disease. In a book of that title, French sociologist Michel Crozier centers the trouble on a faulty American vision of the world, an inability to adapt to changing situations, a permanent mote in the eye caused perhaps by isolation from other continents and peoples. Crozier seems to be unsure whether the disease is acute or chronic: On the one hand we have a chronic Candide tendency to butt our new world heads against old world realities; on the other there is the evidence that Vietnam, Watergate, social tensions, crime, drugs, and the rest are acute symptoms. "The American disease," he writes, "is rooted in the discovery that the limits of development have been reached when Americans thought there were no limits."[20]

It would be wrong to credit foreign sociologists with a monopoly of wisdom or insight. But some of these foreign observations—cited here only as a partial explanation of why Europe today is searching for its own way—are similar to conclusions Americans are reaching themselves. One newspaper, *The Christian Science Monitor,* wrote recently of "an unsettling process started in the 1960s with no end in sight."[21] Some of the causes of the unsettling named by Americans interviewed: television, crime, urban population shifts, family decay, immigration trends, racial injustice, power diffusion in the world. It should be noted that few of these points came up in the 1980 Presidential campaign. Instead, we had a debate centered (again) on the Soviet threat—the decline of American defenses, tax cuts—a debate already three decades old.

But the world has changed dramatically in those three decades. Wrote Crozier:

The bi-polar world of the two superpowers is drawing to a close. . . . We are entering a game of five in which China, Japan and Europe join the two giants—or six with the world of Islam."[22]

And he concludes—not without a soupçon of nostalgia: "There is no more Big Brother."

Notes for Chapter 2

1. Raymond Aron, *Defense de l'Europe Decadent,* (Paris: Robert Laffont, 1977), p. xv.

2. *Ibid.,* p. xvi.

3. A. J. P. Taylor, *The Struggle for Mastery in Europe, 1848–1914* (Oxford: Oxford University Press, 1971), p. 1.

4. Willy Brandt, *People and Politics* (Boston: Little, Brown, 1976), p. 20.

5. Henry A. Kissinger, *The White House Years* (Boston: Little, Brown, 1979), p. 966.

6. Joseph Joffe, "European-American Relations: The Enduring Crisis," *Foreign Affairs,* Spring 1981, p. 845.

7. *The Week in Germany,* January 11, 1980, p. 1.

8. Rudolf Augstein, *Der Spiegel,* January 14, 1980, p. 20.

9. Council on Foreign Relations, *The Soviet Union and the World Economy,* 1977, p. 8.

10. *Times* (London), September 11, 1980, p. 6.

11. Stanley Hoffman, *Primacy or World Order,* (New York: McGraw-Hill, 1978), p. 64.

12. Leonid Brezhnev, speech to Twenty-Fifth Party Congress in Moscow, February 1976.

13. Jean François-Ponçet, private conversation.

14. Dimitri K. Simes, "The Anti-Soviet Brigade," *Foreign Policy* 37 (Winter 1979–1980), p. 30.

15. Hearings before the Committee on Banking, Housing and Urban Affairs, U.S. Senate, October 10, III, 1978, pp. 81–136.

16. Uwe Nerlich, "Change in Europe: A Secular Trend?," *Daedalus,* Winter 1981.

17. William Pfaff, "Reflections: Finlandization," *New Yorker,* September 1, 1980, p. 30.

18. Michael Howard, "Fighting Nuclear War," *International Security,* Spring 1981, p. 8.

19. Robert Jackson, "The Presidential Process," *European Community Magazine,* November–December, 1980, p. 38.

20. Michel Crozier, *Le Mal Americain,* (Paris: Fayard Publishing Company, 1980).

21. *Christian Science Monitor,* January 5–7, 1980.

22. Michel Crozier, *Le Mal American,* 1980.

CHAPTER 3

Lilacs from the Dead Land

> April is the cruelest month,
> Breeding lilacs out of the dead land,
> Stirring dull roots with spring rain,
> Mixing memory with desire.
>
> T. S. ELIOT

WESTERN EUROPE'S RETURN FROM THE WASTELAND of World War II, turning the tables on the United States, is one of the most remarkable economic accomplishments in history. Given the short timespan in which it happened, it may be *the* most remarkable economic achievement in history. The story could be told of Japan as well, but there are differences important enough to merit exclusion of Japan from this account.

The most significant difference was that Japan, a single nation, had no problem of political disunity to overcome. The European accomplishment only became possible because the Europeans were able to overcome a history of antagonism and rivalry and pull their nations together. Separate, the nations of Europe would have remained, even with American aid, middle-sized, post-colonial, resource-poor states. It was their decision to unite that, coupled with the massive infusion of Marshall Plan aid, made the revival so startling.

For a decade following establishment of the EEC in 1957, Europe did not quite know what it had wrought. Exactly ten years later a Frenchman named Jean-Jacques Servan-Schreiber penned a small book called *The American Challenge* in which he stated that not only was the new Europe not working, but its policies were allowing the United States to seize control of the continent industrially, economically, and politically.

Servan-Schreiber's was the story of the old world gradually being taken over by the new in a kind of Darwinian survival of the fittest. Written by a team of writers and economists led by the owner of the newsmagazine *l'Express,* the book sadly told of the Americanization of Europe, how Europe, in a Faustian pact, had bargained its soul for the pleasures of the dollar. Actually, more Schumpeterian than Darwinian, Servan-Schreiber was describing Schumpeter's notion of creative destruction—only on a continental level. Instead of one business devouring another as new products and methods were developed, one continent was taking over from another.

In one unusually mournful passage, Servan-Schreiber wrote:

It seems clear that we Europeans cannot hope to participate fully in the world of the future. This does not mean we will be poor; probably we will grow even richer. But we will be overtaken and dominated, for the first time in our history, by a more advanced civilization.[1]

The book created a shock in France and, as it became known, across Europe. It was a harbinger in the true sense, for until then few people had attempted to describe the long-term effects on Europe of the American-dominated Bretton Woods economic system put in place after World War II. The EEC had been conceived to give Europe the scope and scale to match American power. But ten years after its inception, Europe was dominated from abroad more than ever. Europe's economic recovery was well underway, but it was a recovery that, to Servan-Schreiber, benefitted the United States more than Europe. As Joseph Joffe later would write, "America's investment in Europe paid off beyond all expectations."[2]

This was the Europe the United States had picked up from the ruins. A short twenty years before it lay destitute and impoverished, from Moscow to Paris. The United States, in what would prove to be its grandest piece of post-war foreign policy, moved to the rescue, first with Marshall Plan aid, which would attain more than $14 billion between 1948 and 1952, then with private capital. The economic revival was more spectacular than anything the world had seen before. The British and French, the European victors of World War II, would do well enough, but it was to the vanquished that the real spoils would belong. A German *Wirtschaftswunder* and an Italian economic *miraculo* hoisted these former Fascist enemies to the same level of prosperity as the victors, avoiding the policies of retribution and reparation that followed World War I, and making possible the signing in 1957 of the *Treaty of Rome,* which established the Common Market.

Western Europe, in early 1947, was dying. A wasteland, it stretched from the Memel to the Meuse, a ruin of the crippled and defeated, the destitute and unemployed. Old Europeans still remember the winter of 1946–1947. It was the worst of the century— no fuel for the sheltered and no shelter for the rest. There was no work. For two bitter winter months in 1947 Secretary of State George Marshall sat in Moscow with the foreign ministers of Britain, the Soviet Union, and France trying to find a common policy for this shattered continent. During the deliberations, it became clear that Soviet policy was to let Western Europe rot. "The patient is sinking while the doctors deliberate," Marshall commented.

Russian policy lay naked in the Moscow nights. Just as the nascent Soviet Union had expected revolution to sweep across Germany and Austria following World War I, it expected revolution to come in the devastation of World War II. The *Verelendung*—the poverty and the misery of the working class—would be the vehicle for revolution in Western Europe. How could Moscow be expected to participate in a program for reconstruction, when Communist purposes were to be served by the very ruin itself?

The United States threw its energies and resources into the opposing policy, creating the split that would become the cold war. It would have been hard to defend any other policy. The Marshall Plan may have been, as West German political scientist Uwe Nerlich has said, "improvisation rather than grand design"; still it was foreign policy genius. If the price of the cold war was paying for European reconstruction, it was a price worth paying. As we have seen, it was an investment that paid off handsomely.

When the Marshall Plan was terminated in 1952, American funds continued to flow to Europe in the form of military aid and private capital, accelerating the continent's industrial progress. While American output averaged only a 2.4 percent increase during the 1950s, in Continental Europe it ranged from a low of 3.9 percent in France to 6 percent in Germany. There was one danger sign, however; the British average for the decade was only 2 percent.

From 1946 through 1952, the United States transferred $33 billion to the rest of the world through grants and aid, creating needed liquidity for a world short of funds in which new trading patterns were emerging. The outpour of dollars did not weaken the dollar's value, which under the Bretton Woods system was guaranteed in gold. Though under Bretton Woods we were pledged to redeem foreign-held dollars in gold at $35 an ounce, throughout the 1950s and most of the 1960s the world wanted dollars, not gold. It was the time of a dollar shortage, created by huge new increases in trade, exchange, and investment around the world.

Without these American policies and the dollar to serve them, there could have been no trade expansion, no European recovery, no alternative to the *Verelendung* of the West. Economic policy became the principal instrument of our foreign policy toward Europe. The system seemed ideal for everybody: the United States had almost all the world's gold and could use it to print all the dollars we wanted. The world had an insatiable appetite for dollars and therefore did not redeem them for our gold.

More than dollars alone, however, were needed for the American takeover of Europe described by Servan-Schreiber. The next step, ironically, came in 1957 with the establishment of the European Economic Community and the return of Western European currencies to convertibility. By mid-1957 the dollar, still tightly fixed to gold despite growing balance of payments deficits (and hence already overvalued), could be used freely to purchase European currencies (including the pound, which became convertible at the same time though Britain did not join the Common Market). And used it was. "They are using our money to buy us," Servan-Schreiber would complain.[3] But most Europeans weren't complaining. An Englishman, Angus Maddison, would characterize things this way:

In Continental Europe, the decade of the 1950s was brilliant, with growth of output and consumption, productivity, investment and employment surpassing any recorded historical experience.[4]

But things were not so brilliant for us. The massive one-way capital flow that had lasted for over a decade had begun to erode the real value of the dollar, though the weakness remained hidden by the Bretton Woods guarantees. Nevertheless, by the early 1960s it was apparent that something had to be done. In 1959 the United States trade surplus—which had helped us to pay for the capital outflow—turned into deficit for the first time. Our gold stock fell by $5.1 billion in the years 1958–1960.

The situation worsened throughout the 1960s, particularly in the middle 1960s, precisely the time Servan-Schreiber was writing. If one can fault the Servan-Schreiber analysis, it was on the same grounds one can fault the American analysis of the time: nobody was foreseeing consequences. The Kennedy Administration tried ad hoc measures to help the balance of payments, such as negotiating currency swap agreements with the Europeans and setting up, with them, the London gold pool for regulating gold sales. As early as 1961 President Kennedy had recognized the problem when he told Congress:

The United States must in the decades ahead, much more than at any time in the past, take its balance of payments into account when formulating its economic policies and conducting its economic affairs.[5]

Unfortunately, that sound statement was never translated into policy.

Mere Band-Aids were being used to arrest a dollar hemorrhage, including, ironically, the United States' joining the Marshall Fund. This droll event occurred in 1961 when the Marshall Fund was transformed into something called the Organization for Economic Cooperation and Development (the still-existing OECD), with the United States becoming a full member. A group was set up to deal with the United States deficits. In November 1961 a fund was established for balance of payments financing and $5.8 billion made available for the United States. For the first time since the war our dollars began coming back.

Whatever effect these measures might have had in a situation of *ceteris paribus* cannot be known, for by 1964 we were fighting in Vietnam. Without increasing taxes, President Johnson pressed ahead with the two prongs of his policy—Vietnam and the Great Society. He failed at both, but he succeeded in building permanent inflation into the economy. Defense expenditures went up 25 percent in 1966 and 20 percent more in 1967. The radiator was overheating. Plant utilization at 91 percent in 1966 was the highest since the tranquil Eisenhower year of 1955. Unemployment was at 4 percent; inflation, thanks to cheap energy and the overvalued dollar, was suppressed at 3 percent. Expansion at home pushed up United States imports despite the dollar's strength, accelerating the degradation of our trade balance.

Kennedy had been the first to hit on trade expansion as a means of reducing deficits, and under Johnson the Kennedy Round negotiations with our principal trading partners were concluded. But even this laudable notion was to be counterproductive. Once the negotiations were completed, United States trade balances worsened, thanks primarily to the artificially overvalued dollar, which made our exports expensive, and the undervalued European and Japanese currencies, which made theirs cheap (see Table 1).

We were in a position in which nothing seemed to work. Or, to be more precise, only Murphy's law was working: if things could go wrong, they did. Johnson's efforts to reduce United States direct investment in Europe by restricting outflow of funds not only were ineffective, but, like the trade negotiations, counterproductive. Instead of stopping the outflow of funds, the new measures forced United States companies to move and borrow abroad. The borrowed funds turned out to be dollars owned by European banks *which had been on deposit in the United States.* Our balance of payments worsened!

To meet the new demand for dollars abroad, the European banks transferred funds back to Europe, the genesis of the Eurodollar market. Eurodollars, which amounted to hardly more than $50 billion in 1967, expanded by ten times in the succeeding decade, playing a key role in the world inflation of those years. A solution had become a new problem. The world was afloat on dollars.

TABLE 1

U.S. Balance of Trade, 1961–1979

(in millions of dollars)

Year	Value	Year	Value
1961	+6,001	1971	− 1,465
1962	+5,046	1972	− 5,416
1963	+5,908	1973	+ 1,757
1964	+7,387	1974	− 3,065
1965	+5,716	1975	+ 7,624
1966	+4,532	1976	− 6,078
1967	+4,415	1977	−23,253
1968	+ 990	1978	−23,661
1969	+1,392	1979	−29,469
1970	+3,623	1980	−32,305

Source: U.S. Department of Commerce, Survey of Current Business

So long as there remained a single banana republic banker or anonymous Tyrolean teller who would open an account with no question asked, it was impossible for the world's banking community to assert control over these shifting, undulating, and shadowy dollar balances. Ultimately, they would destroy the dollar's value, a destruction, however, that was implicit in the Bretton Woods system. As economist Robert Solomon has written, the major weakness of Bretton Woods was that it, "failed to provide explicitly for a systematic means by which world reserves could grow with world trade and the world economy."[6] The only system was the dollar.

The classical step in this situation—dollar devaluation—was excluded because of the dollar's fixed link to gold. The Europeans were reluctant to revalue their monies, for this put them at a disadvantage in trade competition with the United States. If they tried

35

to redeem their dollars for gold—something de Gaulle did try—they ran the risk of major political confrontation with Washington. Under President Johnson this flawed system got out of hand. Nothing was to stand in the way of the two national priorities, Vietnam and the Great Society. A cry went up from the more economically rigorous Europeans, who still had to balance exports and imports if they hoped to maintain the value of their monies. Though the Europeans cried, the irony is that they were helped by the situation, which turned out to be disastrous for us.

The dollar's overvaluation, brought about by huge supplies in foreign hands, led to lost markets for us—markets that were gained by West Germans, Japanese, French, and Italians with their undervalued currencies and cheaper prices. They still have many of these markets. By the time of the 1971 Smithsonian agreement devaluing the dollar and eventually severing its link to gold, we were in serious competitive trouble with our major trading partners. The American challenge was about to become the European challenge.

But that is getting ahead of the story. Let us try to recall this Europe of the middle 1960s that Servan-Schreiber was describing. The attempt here is not to be exhaustive, but to give a brief sketch, an economic pencil profile of these nations some two decades after their resuscitation was begun with unprecedented transfers of American wealth, technology, and manpower. Nor should we forget the transfers of taste, style, and culture during the period. The "Americanization" of Europe . . .

ITALY. Italy in the middle 1960s was still living the *miraculo italiano*. Italian economic growth had been rapid and steady throughout the 1950s, faltering only briefly in 1963 and 1964 under the impact of a wage-price explosion that pushed the trade surplus into temporary deficit. It was temporary only. Thanks to a $1 billion emergency loan guaranteed by the United States, Britain, and West Germany, the Italians soon resumed the *miraculo*, and by 1966 some European economists were predicting that Italy would catch France as Western Europe's number-two economy.

Two observations can be made about Italy as it faced the American challenge. First, thanks to extensive government control of the

Italian economy (40 percent of the gross domestic product comes from the government-owned or controlled sector), the American takeover was less pronounced than in Britain or West Germany. Americans invested much less in such major sectors as automobiles, chemicals, oil products, and insurance than they did in other Western European countries.

Second, starting from a lower base than its richer northern neighbors, Italy naturally would grow faster. This would create acute tensions within Italian society. The disparities between rich and poor, city and country, educated and uneducated, farmer and worker, North and South increased and by the 1970s had created contradictions that became a fertile bed for political extremism. Social and economic disjunction led to political instability, keeping the Italians from achieving the kind of social consensus that might have eased their problems.

FRANCE. France, under Charles de Gaulle, who returned to power in 1958 and was re-elected in 1965, showed signs of acute schizophrenia in coping with American economic domination. Under the influence of economist Jacques Rueff, de Gaulle came to believe that Bretton Woods conferred unconscionable political privilege on the United States. Just as he set out to struggle against what he saw as American hegemony in political and military affairs, he set out to do something about the role of the dollar. Throughout the early 1960s the French were steady redeemers of dollars for gold at $35 an ounce.

The French were of different minds concerning direct investment in France by United States companies. During the 1960s French policy underwent several changes, depending frequently on who was running the finance ministry. When General Electric bought a controlling share of Machines Bull, the French computer company, the government moved in and eventually forced GE to sell, lest this key industry of the future be totally dominated by the United States (IBM-France is the nation's largest computer firm).

Though the French became moderately protectionist during de Gaulle's second term, they recognized the fundamental dilemma: "In the short run," Servan-Schreiber wrote, "dependence is beneficial. American investment, though presently an instrument of domination, is also the principal vehicle of technological progress for our economies.''[7] He reached the following conclusion:

In the confusion of today's Europe, France is the country that has shown the most determination not to become a satellite. Some of her reasons have been good, others more dubious. But her frame of reference has been entirely national.[8]

Though the French forced GE to sell Bull, they eventually let Honeywell buy a noncontrolling share of the company.

GERMANY. West Germany had its own *miraculo*—the *Wirtschaftswunder*. The West Germans had come so far so fast under a mixture of Marshall Plan aid, private American investment (by such giants as IBM, Ford, and General Motors), sound economic management, and innate German thriftiness and conservatism that by 1960 the nation was growing at over 8 percent and running substantial surpluses. Peace did for Germany what three wars in the past century had not. So substantial were the surpluses that a first Deutschemark revaluation was carried out in 1961, and Bonn ceased to pay interest on foreign deposits in order to discourage them. Still, the surpluses accumulated as people sought refuge in the currency of a country that seemed responsible and well run.

West Germany, unlike France, did not redeem dollars for United States gold. Bonn may well wish it had. Though West German reserves have climbed over the intervening years, they did not rise as fast as the French (see Table 2). The dollars accumulated by the West Germans were steadily eroded starting in 1961, while the value of the gold held by the French has increased, at this writing, twelvefold over 1971. Bonn's policy of accumulating dollars was not one that could go on forever. It led, during the first years of the Carter Administration, to tension between Bonn and Washington over the value of the dollar. The Germans eventually would warn us that they would no longer go on accumulating a constantly devaluing asset.

What should be retained from the figures in Table 2 are the *relative* changes. The United States still holds more than twice as much gold as any other industrialized country, but we and the British are the only ones who have fallen, while the others are rapidly catching up. The reasons for our fall in gold reserves are similar to those of the British, and they are the classic ones—trade and budget deficits, inflation, falling growth, and productivity rates. *BRITAIN*. Britain, which had been the recipient of American aid back to the prewar lend-lease programs, was a fertile ground for American investment following the war. So quickly did Brit-

TABLE 2

Gold Reserves

(in million of ounces)

	1960	1979	1981
United States	508.7	267.4	264.5
Germany	84.9	94.9	95.2
Switzerland	62.4	83.3	83.3
France	46.9	81.6	81.9
Italy	63.0	66.5	66.7
Japan	7.1	24.0	24.2
Canada	25.3	22.1	21.1
Britain	80.0	18.3	est. 18.7

Source: International Monetary Fund

ain's dollar deficit vanish with Marshall Plan aid that Britain could dispense with it by 1951. With convertibility in 1958, American money began to pour in. It began to look as though American investment would solve the problem of falling productivity that had plagued Britain for a century—what as far back as 1900 the *Times* of London had labeled in a series "The Crisis of British Industry."[9] But what could have been the spark to send Britain back to the forefront of Europe was doused by the government's disastrous political decisions, particularly those that would keep Britain out of the EEC institutions taking shape on the Continent.

In spite of the steadily declining dollar, the worsening situation in Vietnam, and political and social chaos in America, it would have taken considerable foresight in 1967, when Servan-Schreiber wrote, to predict how events would ultimately turn out. The United States, at the time, looked impregnable, able to absorb all shocks and rattle on, relatively unshaken. Our power seemed unaffected by our policies. We were perhaps being nibbled by minnows, but so great was our stature, so unfathomable our resources, and so awesome our economic and military might that we were in a separate class. Servan-Schreiber was attempting an extrapolation, a prediction of the future based on past and existing trends. What he should have done was put on his title page the Latin phrase *rebus sic standibus* recognition that the analysis remained valid only so long as the premises were unchanged. Given the enormous strength of the United States and the still fragile and dependent existence of the European states and their Common Market, it was perhaps impossible to foresee the *renversement des tendences* that would take place. A more prescient analysis, however, far from predicting that the United States would take over Europe, would have detected signs of contradiction.

That is easy to say in retrospect. At the time Servan-Schreiber seemed dead right. Two examples he cited:

• U.S. industry was so overpowering that the profits of General Motors for 1966 equalled the combined profits for that year of the thirty largest German, French, and British firms.

• Among all companies doing more than $1 billion in business for 1966, the United States had sixty and the rest of the world only twenty-seven. We will return to these examples.

Not only was America taking over European business, but it was taking over the Europeans themselves. The best European scientists, businessmen, and doctors flocked to America and American companies. Why go on making $40 per week when you could make five times that and be paid in overvalued dollars to boot? The "brain drain" deprived Europe of its most promising citizens, assuring continued United States technological superiority. So critical did the shortage become in Britain in such professions as medicine and research that the British had to bring in people from the former colonies to replace them. From about 1960 on, if you called on a doctor in London, chances are that he would be a Pakistani, West Indian, or East Indian.

Notes for Chapter 3

1. Jean-Jacques Servan-Schreiber, *The American Challenge* (New York: Avon Books, 1968), p. 65.

2. Joseph Joffe, "European-American Relations: The Enduring Crisis," *Foreign Affairs,* Spring 1981, p. 847.

3. Servan-Schreiber, *The American Challenge,* p. 43.

4. Angus Maddison, *Economic Growth in the West* (New York: Twentieth Century Fund, 1965), p. 25.

5. John F. Kennedy, President's Report to the Congress, Feburary 6, 1961.

6. Robert Solomon, *The International Monetary System, 1945–1976* (New York: Harper & Row, 1977), p. 31.

7. Servan-Schreiber, *The American Challenge,* p. 59.

8. *Ibid.,* p. 139.

9. Peter Jenkins, "Going Down With Britain," *Harpers,* December 1979, p. 24.

CHAPTER **4**

The European Challenge

"We must give the institutions of the European Community the authority, the means and the resources to build a real community capable of adjusting the interests of the member states. This policy is essential if Europe is to be independent of the United States."

PIERRE MENDÈS-FRANCE

FOR THE PAST DECADE or so, nothing has been farther from our minds than Europe. We have been preoccupied with Vietnam, the Soviet Union, China, the Middle East, Afghanistan, El Salvador, the dollar, energy, the recession—not Europe. In a sense, Europe has been an immense bother to us, provoking us, misunderstanding us, opposing us, evoking comments such as Kissinger's "disgusting" about its policy during the Yom Kippur War. Occasionally we have turned on the Europeans as a parent does to a lesser-loved child, gushing attention to slake feelings of neglect. Kissinger did this in 1973 with the unfortunate "Year of Europe," which the Europeans found condescending. In all, we have not known quite what to do with the Europeans. They became too prosperous to treat with political indifference as before, but since they were still less than a superpower, we could not bring ourselves to treat them as equals. They became, quite frankly, a nuisance.

It would be difficult to fix a precise date for the ending of the American challenge to Europe and the beginning of the European challenge to America. Though the turning of the tables didn't become apparent until well into the 1970s, a leg or two was tottering as the 1960s came to an end. Early in the 1970s some prescient people had detected what was happening. A Frenchman named Louis Armand even wrote a short book called, ironically, *The European Challenge*.

Whatever trends were developing in Europe's favor should have been cut short by the oil shock of 1973 and the worldwide recession that followed. As 1974 began, economists were predicting that the growing recession would paralyze Western Europe, cut short its recovery, and reestablish American economic domination over the Continent. More Machiavellian spirits even suggested Washington had engineered the 1973 October war (in which Egypt invaded Israeli-occupied Sinai) in order to increase United States influence in the Middle East and, consequently, the world.

That notion, politically far-fetched, had a degree of logic. The United States had been faltering: Vietnam had ended badly; Watergate was in full cry; the dollar devalued twice. To many it seemed the new oil shortages and higher prices could only help us relative to Western Europe. At the time, we were the world's number-one oil producer, while Europe produced no oil. We had political influence in the Middle East, where Europe was not present. The two most important nations in the Persian Gulf area, Iran and Saudi Arabia, were closely allied to us. Anwar Sadat, who took over in Egypt following Nasser's death in 1970, had expelled some 15,000 Soviet advisers in mid-1972 and was making overtures to the United States to play a more constructive role in the region.

The initial consequences of the energy shortage *did* appear to strengthen the United States at the expense of the Europeans. The American-backed energy conference in Washington in early 1974 showed the Europeans to be disconsolate and divided over their future. A serious Franco-German split developed during the conference, one featured by an open clash between German Chancellor Schmidt and French Foreign Minister Michel Jobert. Jobert, representing French President Georges Pompidou, who was two months from dying, felt the Nixon Administration was using the energy crisis to regain control over Europe by setting up the International Energy Agency, which the French saw as a kind of energy NATO.

The energy penury *should have* reversed the economic trends of the late 1960s and early 1970s. It should have strengthened our economy and currency relative to those of the Europeans. But it did not. As energy prices rose throughout the middle 1970s, so did

United States oil imports. More dollars flooded the world, weakening our currency, which already had slipped seriously following the first devaluation of 1971. From importing 24 percent of our total oil requirements in 1969, imports rose to 47 percent by 1979. Europe, though more dependent on oil imports than we, reduced its dependency during this period. "Why," George Ball would later ask, "was America so tragically slow to comprehend the implication of the massive readjustment in energy costs that began in the aftermath of the Yom Kippur War?"[1]

By the middle 1970s the situation was bleak. Not only had our growth rate tumbled behind the European average again, but so had our rates of savings and investment. According to the OECD, we had fallen to a "historically low savings ratio," 5.1 percent.[2] Savings-and-investment ratios not only are good guidelines for measuring a country's productivity but are an accurate measure of how citizens psychologically view the future. If you are confident, you save more. Lack of confidence leads to more instant gratifications. For 1979, the United States ratio of savings to disposable income was 5.1 percent. For Japan it was 20.5 percent; France, 18.2; Britain, 15.2; Germany, 12.7. Americans lacked confidence in the future, which politically would translate into the Reagan victory over Carter.

There were other ways to measure our economic difficulties following the oil shock. From a period when United States inflation was historically lower than the Europeans, we reached a point in 1978–1981 where we had a rate hardly better than theirs. A three-year average, 1979–1981, looks like Table 1.

Throughout the post-oil shock period our payments and trade balances stayed in deficit, and as oil prices and import levels rose, so did our imbalances, leading to further erosion of the dollar. From an earlier period when the dollar was the world's only reserve currency, other national currencies—the Swiss franc, German mark, British pound, and Japanese yen—began to be held as reserves. Both gold and special drawing rights came into increased use as reserve assets after 1973.

If others did relatively better than we did following the oil shock, it is because they recognized the peril and took action. For trading nations such as Japan and the Western Europeans, nothing is worse than economic imbalance. The oil price increases sent their economies into immediate disequilibrium, and they began a years-long struggle to set things right again. This led, as we shall see, to a panoply of solutions to reduce oil imports.

In the United States, however, a succession of administrations failed to deal with the new situation. International economics and

TABLE 1

Inflation, 1979–1981

(selected OECD countries)

West Germany	4.7 percent
Japan	5.7 percent
France	11.2 percent
United States	11.3 percent
Great Britain	13.2 percent
Italy	16.0 percent

Source: OECD

monetary problems have traditionally taken a back seat in the American political and foreign policy value system, whereas they are first in the priorities of our competitors. It is the disadvantage of being a superpower. *Business Week* described the problem as follows:

To stop the erosion of U.S. power, the country and its leadership in Washington must first recognize that the economic welfare of the United States now depends on how America operates in the international arena. The major problems afflicting the country are all linked together. Their common cause is a fundamentally weak economy that simply cannot compete effectively and pay its own way among the nations of the world.[3]

In November 1978, *in extremis,* monetary measures were taken to correct a situation that had gotten out of hand. Interest rates that would reach 21 percent before Carter left office began to cut into inflation and strengthen the dollar. At the same time, an oil glut showed up that allowed us for the first time since 1974 to cut back oil imports, adding to the dollar's strength. By late 1981 the United States had regained some of the economic edge earlier lost to the Europeans, although the dollar's new cyclical highs threatened to cut short a business recovery that had been fueled by exports when the dollar was low.

It is no longer impossible to generalize about European economic trends. Not too many years ago it was impossible to discuss "European" economics because of the differences among the economies of Britain, Germany, France, and Italy. Prior to 1974, Britain was not a member of the European Community. The three main countries that were in the EEC, West Germany, France, and Italy, all had different economic priorities.

Things have changed. Today the EEC is in the process of harmonizing its economies, bringing the various economic indicators into line so that the Continent gradually becomes a unit, as is the United States, with more-or-less common rates of inflation, growth, unemployment, and interest. Just as the process is far from perfect in the United States, it is imperfect in Europe, but the trends have been right. Throughout the last half of the 1970s the Europeans were able to link their currencies together inside the European monetary system (EMS). Though the election of a Socialist President in France put strains on the EMS, the Europeans' vulnerability to high United States interest rates has reinforced their determination to establish their own monetary system.

Library shelves are thick with volumes comparing French, German, and British economic performance back to the beginning of the industrial age. The books agree on little, other than that economic performances reflect national priorities. The German tendency has been to control inflation. The French predilection has been for full employment and relatively high growth. The British goal has been to achieve an almost unquantifiable notion of "social well-being," which Frenchman Albert Bressand points out curiously enables the economically-troubled British to show up on studies as the "happiest and most optimistic people in Europe."[4]

A novelty is that each of these nations, succeeding in its own way, tends to emulate the others. The French, during the late 1970s, took to imitating the West Germans, controlling inflation and holding down growth. West Germans in the late 1970s tried a little less economic rigor, becoming slightly more "French" in attitude, running higher budget deficits and letting inflation rise. British economist Samuel Brittan even believes the Germans are demonstrating the first symptoms of the "English disease," a kind of creeping sloth.[5] Meanwhile, the British are starting to work again.

Despite national differences, the European economies today have enough in common to be discussed as a unit. Leaving aside Britain, one can say that the main reason Servan-Schreiber turned out to be wrong about the American challenge is that our productivity slipped relative to Europe's. In the decade previous to his writing, from 1957 to 1967 (after the European Marshall Plan spurt), United States productivity was higher than Europe's. Using 1963 as a base year (100) for both, European Community figures show that the United States GNP at market prices was 129 by 1969, while that of the European Nine was 125. Extrapolating from that favorable United States trend and given the absolute United States lead of the time, it was easy for Servan-Schreiber to conclude that the gap, by 1980, would be enormous. Instead, our productivity plummeted over the next decade (see Table 2).

In the economic world there are as many theories about our productivity collapse as there are about the causes of inflation. The most one can conclude is that the causes, like those of inflation, are multiple. Five that are most frequently cited are declining investment, diminishing expenditure on productive research and development, increased government regulation, a decline of manufacturing, and an increasing number of unskilled laborers in the work force. A sixth major cause, which we examine in the next chapter, is defense expenditure.

Different economists put different emphasis on different things. A Presidential report in 1979 found that the root of our productivity problem was falling research and development expenditure and recommended that the government provide the same kind of aid and tax incentives to American industry that the Europeans and Japanese give to theirs.[6] An OECD report, like the Presidential study, singled out the absence of a government incentives policy and an increasingly unskilled work force as the two prime causes of the fall in productivity.[7]

A large body of professional economic opinion holds that the government should take the lead in restoring United States productivity, disagreeing with the current official philosophy that too

TABLE 2

Growth in Real GNP

(percent changes)

	1967–1977	1978	1979	1980
Japan	7.8	5.6	6.0	5.5
West Germany	3.6	3.5	4.2	2.0
France	4.6	3.3	3.0	2.0
United Kingdom	2.1	3.3	.5	−2.2
Italy	4.1	2.6	4.0	3.0
United States	2.8	4.4	2.0	−1.0
Total OECD area	4.2	3.9	3.2	1.1

Source: OECD

much government is the cause of the fall in productivity. Lester C. Thurow of the Massachusetts Institute of Technology has written that "our per capita GNP growth has been higher since the interference-minded New Deal than it was before and the record of other nations offers little support for the laissez faire argument."[8] Indeed, the record of foreign countries shows that their governments today are meticulous in setting national policies to maximize productivity. This takes the form not only of direct aid to export industries, but of socioeconomic programs to smooth the transformation and adaptation of old industry to new products and workers with old skills to new trades. Little is left to chance.

This becomes particularly important as the industrialized world's economies move into a post-industrial phase. As economists Emma

Rothschild and Eli Ginzberg have written, the United States is passing though a period of restructurization in which new industries such as business and building services, health care, and eating and restaurant services are replacing traditional industries of steel, automobiles, and construction.[9] The government role in such a transformation is twofold: to expedite it, easing the way through policies that keep interest and unemployment rates from climbing too high, and to see that federal resources are not squandered on resources that have become nonproductive, such as automobile companies whose cars do not sell and $60 billion missile systems buried in the Nevada desert.

One reason productivity has fallen is that the United States, along with Britain, has entered a post-industrial phase in which manufacturing, construction, and mining no longer dominate the economy. The labor-intensive service industries, with low productivity, are supplanting once-productive classic industries. OECD statistics show that the United States has only 23 percent of its civilian population working in manufacturing, whereas Germany has 35 percent, France 27 percent, and Sweden 25 percent. Of the five major industrial countries—the United States, Japan, Germany, France, and Britain—we have the lowest percentage of the work force in industry.

These statistics suggest that the productivity problem today is endemic and cannot be solved by a simple laissez-faire approach. Curiously, some of the ideas suggested in the OECD study, the MIT report for the President, and Thurow's own work[10]—ideas such as government tax and investment incentives and a national investment committee to aid (when necessary) the economy's best performers and help its worst ones shift into more productive sectors—are already being used by the Japanese and Europeans, who, ironically, adopted them years ago to help their industries match American productivity.

From a time when the newer industrialized nations of Western Europe and Japan admired our laissez-faire business practices and emulated them, we have reached a point at which their more paternalistic methods are proving to be more productive. Sociologist

Michel Crozier writes of the "devaluation of the American worker" through stop-go business methods that fluctuate between massive hirings and layoffs—and reduce productivity. The great strength of German and Japanese industry, he writes, is its specialized work force, "hired, trained and protected with loving care." [11] West Germany, with an apprentice system that directs high school graduates into 450 separate, government-classified occupations, has drastically reduced youth unemployment in that country. Following Britain's urban riots of mid-1981, the Thatcher government began to implement a program resembling the German one.

The conservative contradiction in America today is to believe that government is the cause of a problem that others now believe government must take the lead in solving. If the others are right, the Reagan phenomenon, so understandable in political terms, will be sociologically and economically disastrous unless we quickly learn that pre-industrial economics will not work for post-industrial problems. If America indeed has entered a phase of low or no growth, the government is likely to have a greater role to play, particularly in assuring that special-interest groups and privileged segments of society do not appropriate socially unjustifiable portions of diminishing resources.

This may mean, as we have seen in Britain, the government's acting to break the stranglehold of a too-powerful member of society, in this case, British labor unions; it may mean, as in the case of Japan and Germany, the government's acting to assure that national consensus is established among the principal groups of society, in this case, labor, business, and government. It may mean, as in the case of most of the Western Europeans, the government's legislating new programs to minimize the social cost of economic transformation. It may mean that, for the first time, we come to terms with the economic cost of military expenditure.

Let us specifically examine some European approaches to the productivity problem. The Europeans have, to be sure, more freedom of action than we. Smaller, more sociologically homogeneous, their social programs are more efficient. Not being superpowers, they are not burdened by military expenditure, which are notoriously nonproductive. In the economic battle between guns and butter, they more frequently can opt for butter. (The classic economic comparison, guns and butter, is no longer a very good one, since if anything is as wasteful as producing guns, it probably is butter. A better choice would be between guns and transistors). We won't dally too long over the smallest European countries— Scandinavia and the Benelux countries. Historically given few world or regional responsibilities, these nations have been content to keep low international profiles and get on with the construction of welfare societies, usually balanced somewhere between structural capitalism and functional socialism. The difference between them and market socialist countries such as Yugoslavia and (increasingly) Hungary and Poland is that the means of production remain in private hands. The government's role is essentially one of regulation and redistribution (through fiscal policy) of the fruits of production.

The risk run by these small nations is twofold. It may be, in the long run, that cradle-to-grave security deprives the population (at least parts of it) of the kind of innovative energy (and higher productivity) that comes from personal insecurity. The solution is to strike the right balance: enough personal security through entitlements such as health care, job insurance, and free education so that innovative energy is liberated rather than stifled.

It may be that some of these smaller countries already have reached the limits of the welfare state. As the 1980s got underway, conservative political reactions had set in in most of them, essentially aimed at holding the welfare state where it was, even trimming it. By 1980, the countries of Benelux and Scandinavia were paying close to 50 percent of their national incomes to the government in taxes. The conservative reaction was aimed at keeping the percentage from climbing higher, something which would threaten the capitalist base.

The four biggest nations of Western Europe—in order of population—West Germany (61 million), Italy (57 million), Great Britain (56 million), and France (53 million) have not felt free to go quite so far as the smaller countries in the trade-off between entitlements and defense, welfare and capitalism. But each has gone farther than the United States, and the gap widened during the 1970s. Each has established certain basic social minimums that include such programs and policies as free health care, free secondary and university education for all qualifying students, direct family subsidies, retirement insurance, comprehensive unemployment insurance and job retraining, rigorous legislation for job layoffs and dismissals, nationalization of essential industries that have become

TABLE 3

Government Expenditure

(as percentage of GNP)

Belgium	42.7	Netherlands	54.4
Canada	35.8	Norway	52.1
Denmark	46.5	Sweden	60.1
France	42.3	Switzerland	34.0
Germany	43.3	United Kingdom	38.8
Italy	37.4	United States	32.6
Japan	24.3		

Source: *OECD Observer*, March 1980

unprofitable (principally in transportation), and legal minimums for vacations and holidays (generally five weeks). To pay for these programs, each of these nations (as well, obviously, as the smaller ones) pays a high portion of its national income to the government in taxes (see Table 3). The exception to the rule is Japan, where most of the responsibility for the welfare of the worker lies not with government but with the employer.

Western Europe today is searching for a third way, one somewhere between the extremes of the Soviet model, with its domination of the individual by the state, and the American one, with its domination of the state by the individual. If the Soviet way clearly never was a model for Europe, the American way once was. It is no longer. As financier Felix Rohatyn has put it: "The examples of Germany and Japan should convince us that a genuine partnership of business and labor in government is required to accomplish any program dealing with inflation and the economy.''[12]

Let us look at another example of the turning of the economic tables during the 1970s. When Servan-Schreiber wrote, the flow of direct investment between Europe and the United States was one way. Though Europeans and others held significant assets in the United States, they were in the form of dollar deposits, equities, and credit instruments. Lacking technology and methodology, Europe showed relatively little interest in taking over United States companies.

United States direct investment in Western Europe increased steadily during the 1950s and 1960s. From $2.5 billion in 1955, it reached $25 billion in 1970, $38 billion in 1973, and $80 billion by 1979. While these totals are for Western Europe as a whole, 70 percent of the investment went into the ten countries that today make up the EEC.[13]

The concentration of investment in specific sectors increased its effectiveness. In 1967, the year Servan-Schreiber wrote, United States direct investment in Western Europe totalled $18.2 billion. Of that amount, $4 billion was in petroleum, $3 billion in machinery and equipment, $2 billion in transport, and $1.8 billion in chemicals. The concentration often led to near-monopoly control. Situations were established that still exist today. One could read recently that ''International Business Machines Corporation is casting a darker shadow than ever over the West European computer industry.''[14] Not only does IBM control 53 percent of the West European computer industry today, but American companies control 87 percent of its semiconductor business. Servan-Schreiber's error was to generalize from such individual examples.

If the United States dominates European computers and semiconductors, we find the Europeans (and Japanese) returning the favor and taking greater control in such classic American industries as automobiles, electronics, textiles, shoes, steel, shipbuilding, merchandising, and transportation. The fall in the value of the dollar in the 1970s was the key to the takeover. In a sector such as surface transportation, a more sophisticated European and Japanese analysis of energy trends enabled them to make sizable inroads into the market. By 1980, Volkswagen was producing its fuel-efficient Rabbits in one $350 million Pennsylvania plant and planning another $225 million plant in Michigan. Renault had taken over American Motors, Peugeot was buying into Chrysler, and Honda was opening up a $200 million plant in Ohio. In case they needed tires, Michelin had invested $200 million in radial tire plants in South Carolina and Texas.

The European takeovers came so fast that the days when Americans used to protest foreign ownership—recall the flap over Rothschild Bank's purchase of Pittsburgh's Copperweld in 1975—seemed part of another era, as indeed they were. Today it is Flick buying into W. R. Grace; Elf-Aquataine buying Texas-Gulf; Thyssen taking over Budd; Schlumberger buying Fairchild Camera; the Imperial Group buying Howard Johnson; Flick (again) buying into U.S. Filter; Bayer taking up Miles Laboratories; Phillips taking Magnavox. European banks took over Crocker National, Union Bank, and CIT Finance; European oil companies took interests in Sinclair Oil and Sohio. The list goes on.

With their more sophisticated transport industry and long-term perspective, the Europeans were particularly keen on the American transport industry. A. G. Thyssen's purchase of Budd, a leading producer of rolling stock, put that West German company in a strong position to cash in on the eventual revival of United States railroads. When an $86 million all-trolley urban transit system started up in San Diego in 1981—the first all-trolley system built in the United States in 30 years, West German streetcars were on the rails. By 1979 total direct investment by the United States in Europe had reached $80 billion, but, with the trends in their favor, direct European investment in the United States had climbed to $40 billion. During both 1979 and 1980 foreign investment in the United States ran ahead of American investment abroad. In 1979 and 1980 European investment in the United States doubled in annual rate over the previous year.

The figures for West Germany were particularly dramatic. At the end of 1978 the United States had $12.7 billion directly invested in West Germany, and the West Germans only $3.2 billion in the United States (direct investment is ownership of more than 10 percent of a corporation). By mid-1980, however, West German Ministry of Economics figures showed that a surge in investment over the preceding eighteen months had lifted direct German holdings in America to $11.2 billion against corresponding United States ownership in Germany of $12.9 billion—a remarkable change in less than two years.

Some Americans were worried. "The bottom line," said Congressman Benjamin S. Rosenthal during a House subcommittee hearing on foreign investment in the United States, "is that more and more decisions about our economy may be made outside the United States. That's vulnerability."[15] Although some short-term advantage existed in importing foreign funds to help meet our chronic payments' deficits, the long-term trends were worrisome. Eventually, the return on capital to the foreign investors would surpass the influx of new capital to us. The reversal of Atlantic investment trends in the late 1970s was a demonstration of how much of America's economic power had flowed to the other side of the Atlantic in a decade. The American Challenge of the 1960s had become the European Challenge of the 1980s.

The rise of Western Europe as an economic power in the 1970s had several explanations, not all of them connected to the political and economic difficulties of the United States. Western Europe always has had the potential to perform in a more unified and coherent manner, but, rent by division and rivalry, it generated more motion than movement. Britain's membership in the EEC in 1974 put an end to the long struggle between the Continent and the Island and created an economic market population of 250 million. But it remained for the Europeans to deal with severe structural, institutional, and political weaknesses before they could emerge as a unified economic power rather than simply a group of semiprosperous rival states.

One historic problem had been the lack of economic scale. The creation of the EEC in 1957 provided a framework for solving this problem by giving the original six members free trade access to the markets of the others. The arrival of Britain extended this to a nine-nation area (Denmark and Ireland joined at the same time). The figures tell the story. If we recall Servan-Schreiber's example, in 1966 the United States had sixty firms with annual sales of more than $1 billion; the rest of the world counted only twenty-seven. Today, the United States has forty-nine firms doing more than $6 billion annual business (a roughly corresponding figure to $1 billion), while the rest of the world has fifty-four, most of them Western European.[16] The Western Europeans have been combining and merging, nationally and internationally, for well over a decade now, forming in many cases cartels that would be illegal in America.

Only a decade ago Western Europe was a continent distinguished largely by economic duplication, waste, and inefficiency. If companies survived, they did so on the basis of quality and originality, certainly not profitability derived from scale. Their largely artisanal approach to production came severely under attack during the 1970s when much of what they were doing in traditional industries such as steel, textiles, automobiles, photography, electronics, apparel, and shipbuilding began to be duplicated—at lower prices— by the increasingly prosperous developing nations and by Japan. The Western Europeans found themselves squeezed by the economic scale of the Americans on one side and the cost efficiency of the Asians on the other. They responded to the challenge through merger, cartels, joint venture, and higher productivity.

It is almost impossible to keep up with European industrial mergers today. From a time when European industry was atomized and easily dominated by Japanese or American firms, they have combined into their own transnational companies today, able to compete in scale with other giants. The Europeans have combined or are combining today in the following sectors: computers, nuclear energy, chemicals, aeronautics, electronics, banking, steel, textiles, photography, heavy equipment, automobiles, food processing, and engineering. Europe today has industries that are "national" in the sense that ours are national. As one European has put it: "One of the aims is to foster the emergence of firms that could be described as European in the same sense that Mitsubishi is Japanese."[17]

Just as the Europeans learned from us the technique of using our own money to purchase us, they have adapted our management and business techniques for use in the competition. This is how *Fortune* magazine described it:

The Europeans feel they have enhanced American management techniques with skills and advantages of their own. Lacking a huge home market, European managers learn foreign languages as a matter of course, and their companies are extremely export-minded. As a result, they adapt readily to strange surroundings.[18]

European industry has yet another advantage over ours. With its predominantly owner-appointed managements, European companies have developed closer owner-management relations than have American companies, whose stocks are increasingly owned by large institutions. Some analysts believe the growing divorce between ownership and management of large United States corporations is still another prime cause of falling United States productivity. Large institutional stockholders, their studies show—pension funds, mutual funds, and insurance companies—are primarily interested in short-term profits, the "bottom line," rather than long-term growth and higher productivity, which is emphasized in Europe.

Notes for Chapter 4

1. George Ball, "Reflections on a Heavy Year," *Foreign Affairs,* Vol. 59, No. 3, p. 477.
2. OECD, *Economic Outlook,* December 1979, pp. 79, 119.
3. The *Business Week* Team, *The Decline of U.S. Power* (Boston: Houghton-Mifflin, 1980), p. 201.
4. Albert Bressand, "The New European Economics," *Daedalus* 108, (Winter 1979), p. 66.
5. Samuel Brittan, "The English Malady Proves Contagious," *Financial Times,* November 23, 1980, p. 16.
6. See Pergamon Policy Studies, *Technological Innovation for a Dynamic Economy* (Elmsford, New York: Pergamon Press, 1979).
7. OECD, *Survey of United States Economy,* 1979, p. 24.
8. Lester C. Thurow, "Are There Solutions For Our Economic Problems?", *New York Times,* August 10, 1980, p. 32.
9. Emma Rothschild, "Reagan and the Real America," *New York Review of Books,* February 5, 1981, p. 12; Eli Ginzberg, "The Service Sector of the U.S. Economy," *Scientific American,* March 1981, p. 48.
10. See Lester C. Thurow, *The Zero-Sum Society,* (New York: Basic Books, 1980).
11. Michel Crozier, *Le Mal Americain,* (Paris: Fayard Publishing Comapny, 1980), p. 273.
12. Felix Rohatyn, "The Coming Emergency and What Can Be Done About It," *New York Review of Books,* December 4, 1980, p. 24.
13. U.S. Department of Commerce, *Survey of Current Business,* August 1979, p. 15.
14. "European Strategies to Fight IBM," *Business Week,* December 17, 1979, p. 73.
15. *New York Times,* August 8, 1980.
16. *Fortune,* May 5, 1980, pp. 276–277; August 11, 1980, pp. 190–192.
17. Bressand, "The New European Economics," p. 64.
18. "Europe Outgrows Management American Style," *Fortune,* October 20, 1980, p. 148.

CHAPTER 5

Oil and Iron

"It is a fact that since 1969 the Department of Defense has underestimated the costs of all major weapons systems by more than 50 percent."
Hearings before a Subcommittee of the House Committee on
Government Operations, 1979

ANY COMPARISON of America's economic performance over the past two decades with those of other industrialized nations must center on oil and iron (defense spending). These two costs have become so important as to dwarf others; no analysis of our economic decline can fail to give them prime roles. Oil imports today cost Americans over $100 billion annually, an amount about equal to Australia's gross national product. Defense spending today runs about $200 billion per annum, heading for $300 billion, which will be close to a third of our federal budget and more than 7 percent of our national income. Inherently wasteful and inflationary, defense expenditure rises so rapidly that it is impossible to forcast replacement costs for today's equipment.

While defense expenditure undermines the domestic economy, oil import costs work primarily against us in an international environment, that is, weaken our currency and our diplomacy. Our annual $100-billion bill counts against our trade balance and hence is out-of-pocket. To make up for the bill—the equivalent of a $500 annual foreign tax on each American—our industry and agriculture must perform Herculean export labors in return. This foreign tax on us can be raised at will, and is. Semiannually the ministers of the Organization of Petroleum Exporting Countries (OPEC) meet to decide how much the tax will be raised. It is the most flagrant kind of taxation without representation since King George III applied the stamp and sugar taxes. But while our ancestors had the good sense to refuse to pay the foreign tax, we go ahead, unwilling to take the steps they did to end an equally intolerable and far more dangerous situation.

OIL

Dependence on imported oil for almost half our consumption is the most serious economic problem America has faced since the Depression. In its potential it is worse than the Depression, for the political consequences of foreign economic dependence in the nuclear age are incalculable. Our future today is in the hands of Persian Gulf Bedouin families. Policy has become the creation of "emergency reserves" and formation of rapid deployment forces to keep these families in power if ever they are threatened by other families that would not sell us their oil or by nationalistic forces similar to those that turned against the Shah of Iran. There can be no doubt that the seeds of future world conflict are being sown today—not in Europe, where three decades of Americans have expected eventual trouble, but in the Persian Gulf.

The vacuum that the Gulf represents today will be filled. And since it cannot be filled by local power—including, as should now be evident to everyone, Iraq—it will be filled by outside power. This can only mean that it will be controlled either by the United States, or by the Soviet Union or by a condominium of the two superpowers.[1]

Professor Robert Tucker, author of these lines, a man who has been prolific in his writings on American contingency planning for military occupation of the Persian Gulf, does not really believe we should reach a new Yalta accord with Moscow to divide up the Gulf region. It should belong to us alone:

All this is so clear that it is tedious to place such emphasis on it. Yet the conclusions that must be drawn from the virtually self-evident still appear to escape many. And the principal conclusion is simply that the center of gravity of American interests in the world today is not to be found in Europe but in the Persian Gulf.[2]

61

One's tendency might be to dismiss such notions as fantastic if they did not, by virtue of not being taken seriously, seem to be gaining ground. An interventionist tendency, not overpowering but vigorous, persists among Americans who have not digested the lessons of the 1960s and 1970s. The American experiences in Vietnam and Iran, the Soviet experiences in China, Indonesia, and Egypt should be demonstrations that interventionism today is not productive policy. In the short run it may be tempting and even provide illusory gain, but in the long run it is self-destructive. How much worse off would we be today if in 1953 the Central Intelligence Agency had not intervened in Iran to bring down Mohammed Mosaddegh and reinstall the Shah on the throne?

The notion that a pernicious dependence on Persian Gulf oil somehow transforms those desert duchies into the "center of gravity" for American interests is akin to saying that the vital interest for the drug addict is the dope peddler. Sanity is not the habit but kicking it. If the possibilities for withdrawal are not immediate, as they are not for us, then we must do what we can to stay on decent terms with the suppliers as we go about straightening things out. This does not mean adopting the kind of policy we did in Iran, which was to sustain an unpopular and corrupt regime to the bitter end, when all national forces had turned against it. Ultimately we paid the price. Or, to be exact, fifty-two compatriots, taken hostage in Iran, paid the price for us.

The foreign policy debate today over the relevance of the Persian Gulf to American interests is not so complex as sometimes is presented. The facts are these: the United States (plus Western Europe and Japan) has developed a valuable trade relationship with the oil kingdoms of the Persian Gulf. Just as trading nations throughout history have had the right to protect their trade lanes from foreign interference—whether from Barbary Coast piracy or Wahhabi rebelry—we have the right today to protect ours. For this we need a strong Navy. What makes the situation different from a century ago is that the age of imperialism has run out. These trading regions no longer are Western outposts in vast imperiums but sovereign nations banded together with like-minded nations into powerful economic and political cartels. OPEC is an example of such a group. Our trade relationship with these nations must today be based on mutual agreement and self-interest, and this, to be durable, must be based on national consensus on both sides.

Two complications are present in the America-Gulf trade arrangement: First, we have become so dependent that our policy has become one of desperation. The American economy could be brought to a halt by still unknown sheiks yet to wander out of the Ar-rab al-Khali. This has led to the mistaken ideas of Professor Tucker, the Reagan administration, James Schlesinger, and others that we need American soldiers to preserve local regimes in power. The second complication is found in the proximity of the Persian Gulf to Russia. Despite recent experience, the United States maintains a propensity to see nationalistic upheavals almost anywhere as controlled by the hand of Moscow. We are still waiting for Iran to go Communist.

The American confusion over the difference between the rise of nationalism and Soviet expansionism has caused us considerable grief over the past two decades. In the Gulf region it has disastrous implications. For what possible reason should we believe that turning Saudi Arabia, Egypt, Oman, or Yemen into American anti-Communist bases would turn out better than similar exercises in Vietnam or Iran? The record shows that such activity accelerates the process of decomposition. Nothing serves as a lightning rod for nationalism more than foreign bases, American or Soviet.

We would be doing our friends in Egypt or Saudi Arabia no favor by establishing American bases on their soil. In the age of nationalism, if the perception gains ground that a regime can be sustained only by outside interference, that regime can begin counting its days. Outside interference will polarize national sentiment against the interfering "friend" and play into the hands of opposing ideological and political forces. The Soviet Union can be no more secure in Afghanistan than we were in Iran. The Saudis have so far rightly refused to base American troops. Before we put them into Egypt we should ask ourselves why Egypt wants them, if indeed it does. Even the security-conscious International Institute of Strategic Studies has raised doubts about the troops: "The strain on regional politics caused by such a deployment could outweigh the military benefit derived from deterring Soviet threats," it wrote.[3]

The difference between American policy in the Persian Gulf and the policies of our allies is illuminating. Both the Europeans and Japanese have shown clearer instincts for dealing with the diffusion of power over the last two decades than we. Neither has accepted the interventionist argument that the Soviet Union is the principal danger in the Persian Gulf. Neither has shown any inclination to solve Persian Gulf political problems either with militaristic bluster or by confusing religious or nationalist tendencies with Soviet expansionism. Both the Europeans and Japanese are taking the realistic step of beginning to reduce oil dependence—not on the grounds that the oil should go to someone else, but on the sensible grounds that too much dependence is bad economics and bad politics. The West Germans, as we have seen, are turning to the Russians for natural gas in order to reduce their Persian Gulf dependence. As one European commentator has asked, forced to choose between Saudi Arabia and the Soviet Union as a long-term source of oil supply—"Which source do you think is likely to prove more dependable?"[4]

The key to maintaining the Persian Gulf region as a long-term source of reduced Western oil supply is to end the confusion between nationalism and Communism and to attempt to stay on good terms with the seller nations—no matter what regime comes to power. Our interest is with nations, not regimes. Our error is to become so compromised with one particular faction, propping it up illegitimately, that when another takes over it no longer is willing to trade with us. We had no business plotting to keep the Shah in power when his whole nation had turned against him. Certainly the history of the oil-rich states teaches that they will do business with anybody who has dealt with them honorably. These states are not lusting for communism. As Alistair Horne notes in his brilliant history of the Algerian war, "the bogey slogan of the Soviet fleet at Mers-el-Kebir retained its force right until the last days of the French presence."[5]

The same holds true of Libya. The United States was not compromised with the regime of former King Idris and found that when he was ousted by Colonel Moammer Qaddafi, even these new pan-Arab fundamentalists continued to be reliable exporters of oil to us. Even pan-Arab fundamentalists need dollars.

The figures in Table 1 show that the United States was the only major industrialized nation to increase dependence on imported oil between 1973 and 1979. We earned the lowest OECD rating of all industrialized countries for energy consumption during those years.

TABLE 1

Net Imports of Oil

(in millions of barrels per day)

	1973	1974	1975	1976	1977	1978	1979	1980
United States	6.2	6.4	6.0	7.3	8.7	8.0	8.0	6.7
Japan	4.9	4.8	4.3	4.6	4.8	4.7	4.8	5.0
France	2.5	2.4	2.0	2.3	2.1	2.1	2.2	2.5
Germany	2.8	2.6	2.4	2.6	2.6	2.7	2.7	2.7
Italy	1.9	1.9	1.7	1.8	1.7	1.7	1.7	2.0
United Kingdom	2.2	2.1	1.7	1.5	1.0	0.8	0.3	0.2

Source: OECD and American Petroleum Institute

We used a quarter more energy than we produced. Though there was a drop in the quantity of oil imported during 1980—thanks to higher domestic production, higher prices, and an economic recession—the improvement was only relative. Though we purchased less, we paid more for it, as the average imported price went from $19.81 per barrel in 1979 to $31.89 in 1980. Said the OECD:

Not only does the United States put disturbingly large claims on the world's energy resources, but the relative size of the United States consumption and its energy policies (makes) it more difficult for other countries to adopt effective energy policies.[6]

Although there has been no consensus among other industrialized states on how to deal with OPEC oil prices, their different policies have led to the same results: fewer imports. All have been helped by the ability of their governments to make and enforce energy policy, something America, with our government by stalemate, was not able to do. For some—Japan, Italy, West Germany, and France are the best examples—the effort was great, for they have no domestic oil. For them, the goal has been to reduce oil consumption without destroying economic growth, and some have been remarkably successful.

The United States produces over three-quarters of the energy it consumes, whereas a nation such as Japan produces less than a quarter of its consumption. Between 1973 and 1979, however, Japan reduced its oil imports and increased its domestic energy production, while American trends were in the opposite direction. The Japanese reductions were mirrored by those of other nations. Improvements for all the importing nations were shown in 1980, with the aid of a mild winter, and as higher prices began significantly to discourage consumption.

For Japan the means primarily have been conversion to coal and liquified natural gas. In 1980, while industrial production was rising by 7 percent, oil consumption was falling by 10 percent.[7] The oil Japan imports now comes from diversified sources, including increasing amounts from Mexico. Twenty-one nuclear plants are now in operation, a figure that is to be doubled in this decade.

France is the nuclear leader of the world, having become in 1980 the first country to derive 20 percent of total electricity from nuclear power. The government's plan calls for nuclear power to reach 30 percent of total energy by 1990, with natural gas and oil each supplying another 30 percent.[8] Whether these goals are reached under the Socialists is another matter, but there is no doubt about France's commitment to nuclear energy as a means of escaping oil dependence. France is a world leader both in fast-breeder and plutonium reprocessing technology.

The West German approach has been unique. Hampered to a greater degree than France by anti-nuclear movements, the Germans have turned to other technologies, particularly coal gasification, in which they have become the leader. Though Germany has not been able to reduce total oil consumption as a percentage of total energy beyond the 51 percent reached in 1978, the Germans are diversifying their suppliers and in 1980 imported 41 percent of their oil needs from Africa, 14 percent from the North Sea, 3.2 percent from the Soviet Union, and increasing amounts from Mexico.[9] West Germany has become the largest importer of British oil, an arrangement which has helped balance Britain's trade figures with the Continent's strongest economy. Bonn today buys 16 percent of its natural gas from the Soviet Union and over half of its enriched uranium, with both amounts rising. These changes in traditional energy patterns, diversifying away from Persian Gulf dependence, have strengthened European political and economic ties, both West-West and East-West.

Italy, a country with high dependence on foreign oil, like Japan, is switching from oil to natural gas. Italy is a major purchaser of Soviet natural gas and is completing a trans-Mediterranean pipeline that will being North African natural gas directly on line. In addition, Italy imposes the highest tax on gasoline sales, which is another means of reducing consumption. Some typical gasoline tax rates in 1980: United States, 15 cents per gallon; United Kingdom, 89 cents; West Germany, $1.14; France, $1.62; Italy, $1.83.

What has been American policy compared with these of our leading competitors? Here are the conclusions of the Harvard Energy Project:

The United States is at the center of the world oil problem, having failed to come to grips with the decline of its influence over the world petroleum market and the *true costs of its oil imports*. By allowing its citizens to receive $15 billion in subsidies to use oil and by ignoring the *even larger external costs associated with imported oil,* the United States has been encouraging a form of behavior that will drain the world of the commodity [my italics]. This is a reckless course, increasing the vulnerability of the entire Western world and undermining the leadership of the United States within it. In short, increasing dependence on imported oil poses a threat to American political and economic interests; that much must now be clear.[10]

Few Americans would fault the conclusions of the Harvard Business School. The Carter Administration was strong on ideas but lacked the ability to get programs through Congress. Its boldest attempt would have imposed a 10 percent fee on oil imports, passing the tax on to consumers through a gasoline tax. It was defeated. Carter's oil quota plan would have fixed imports at 1977 maximums, the highest in our history, a meaningless gesture. Carter did begin a phased deregulation of domestic natural gas and crude oil prices to encourage more domestic exploration. He also passed a windfall profits tax to keep all the benefits of higher oil prices from going to the oil industry, which already accounts for 40 percent of total manufacturing profits.

The Reagan Administration's energy program is based on the free market principle that if you leave the oil industry alone it will find more oil. It is sound enough policy so long as the oil is there, but the Harvard report disputes that it is. The rapid rise of OPEC prices, however, has begun to make the production of domestic shale oil competitive, and oil experts today estimate that with increased shale production, total American oil production will remain at current levels of 10 million barrels per day throughout the 1980s despite the decline in existing fields. It is obvious that maintaining existing levels of domestic production does nothing for reducing foreign dependence.

The rise of domestic oil and gasoline prices through decontrol of prices already has led to significant reductions in foreign imports, from over 8 million barrels per day to 7 million. One sound option for this country would be to fix a mandatory import limit today at a level that would keep imports from rising above present levels. A mandatory quota fixed at, say, 7.5 million barrels would have strong psychological impact and do nothing to crimp the economy. It would be psychologically coercive without the harmful physical effects of quotas—which deplete domestic reserves, lead to inefficient allocation, and provide a windfall benefit for importers.

It is neither possible nor desirable for America to become energy *independent*. President Nixon's "Project Independence," which would have made us energy independent by 1981, not only was impossible but was poorly inspired policy. In an interdependent trading world we have an interest in the comparative advantage of oil economics, as does any country for any commodity. The goal today should be to moderate our dependence, bring it back to the politically and economically acceptable levels of the 1960s. We can not afford today to import almost half of our oil at prices fifteen times higher than a decade ago.

IRON

It is regarded as perverse to discuss security and defense in economic terms. Defense specialists prefer to believe that security has no price and that the best way to avoid war is to prepare for it. Unfortunately, as Lord Mountbatten noted shortly before his death, the age of strategic missiles and nuclear warheads has made nonsense of both these notions. Security has a price today, one that rises so fast that it literally prices weapons out of the market. The antiballistic missile system, which both the United States and Soviet Union renounced in the first SALT treaty, was one such weapon. The MX missile is probably another. As for avoiding war by preparing for it, history offers no precedents for the kind of nuclear stockpiles we have acquired today. On the other hand, one can think of few times in history where such extravagant accumulations of arms have not eventually led to war—which is what makes arms control so important today.

Different countries in different ways are coming to terms with today's high cost of defense. Britain had to renounce its role as a world power because it no longer could afford what it cost. There are some in Britain today (including the conservative magazine *The Economist*) who would give up Britain's strategic submarine nuclear deterrent and save the $10 billion to be spent on the American-made Trident submarines, an expense which the 1980–1981 *Jane's All the World's Aircraft* called a "stupidity." West Germany cut back on its 1981 commitment to NATO because money was not available to pay increased costs. Israel, Egypt, Turkey, Portugal, and innumerable Third World countries have discovered that they could spend themselves into bankruptcy with defense. The Soviet Union, as we will see, finds its economic growth permanently crippled by its security obsessions. The focus here is on the economic not the military side of defense.

The problem, simply stated, is that no costs are as inflationary and unproductive as military costs. That may sound like a truism, but as James J. Treires has noted, "the close relationship between big military budgets and inflation escapes notice or commentary by most of the major news media."[11] Recent studies have shown that defense expenditures increase about five times as fast as the consumer price index. In one twelve-month period alone in 1979–1980, the prices of planes acquired by the United States Marines rose 35 percent, of tracked vehicles by 46 percent, and of boats and ships by 57 percent. As Lieutenant General Paul X. Kelley has testified, the Marines were forced to reduce manpower by 10,000 men during that period to pay the increased equipment costs, substituting machines for men,[12] a dangerous precedent.

The defense industry today is a major cause of the inflation endemic to our society. With price increases vastly above those of the consumer price index, defense exerts a steady upward pull on all prices. Since all defense costs are paid by the government (i.e., by the public), they lead to bigger federal budgets, higher deficits, increased taxes, and higher interest rates. As President Reagan will discover, there is no socially acceptable way to increase defense spending, cut taxes, balance the budget, and reduce inflation.

New studies show defense spending has played a key role in the decline of American industrial productivity. Both the MIT and OECD studies discussed in Chapter 4 stress the economic disadvantage inherent in military spending. The OECD report specifically recommends that research and development funds be moved out of "pure" technology—that is, defense—and channeled into areas of manufacture and marketing where the impact on the economy is greater.

These conclusions are not different from those of Seymour Melman in his seminal study of military spending and its effect on the economy. The MIT and OECD reports and a new book by the Boston Study Group use more recent data to reinforce Professor Melman's basic conclusion. Melman stated that:

The decline of the United States as an economic and industrial system is now well underway. This is the consequence of the normal operation of a thirty-year military economy fashioned under government control at the side of civilian capitalism. The new state-controlled economy, whose unique features include *maximization of costs and of government subsidies,* has been made into the dominant economic form in American capitalism [my italics].[13]

What Melman called the "cost maximization work habits of the defense industry" was responsible for a large part of the drop in American productivity. When the object of a contract is not to reduce costs but to increase them, when there is no "bottom line" and no salesroom competition, the constraints of the marketplace are effectively removed.

One of the ironies of Ronald Reagan's election was that his campaign slogan of "getting the government off the backs of industry" was totally inconsistent with his plans for increasing the defense budget—a prime cause of our industry's troubles. America's productive industry already is penalized by the loss of many of its best engineers to the defense sector, whereas in Europe and Japan these workers are employed in the productive sector. As Nobel-Prize-winning economist Wassily Leontief has stated, handled improperly, "these huge jumps in U.S. military spending will mean higher inflation, a worsening balance of payments, a drain on productive investment, soaring interest rates, increasing taxes, a debased currency and, in the long term, more unemployment."[14]

It once was believed that funds spent on military research and development had a positive impact on the civilian economy. Current studies dispute this, suggesting that defense funds are too narrowly employed to have much fallout effect on civilian productivity. The foreign experience seems to confirm this. Japan, which has no defense industry and is prohibited by its constitution (the 1947 MacArthur constitution) from "the threat or use of force as a means of settling international disputes," has the highest productivity of all industrial nations.

In a recent report the Defense Commission of the French National Assembly reported that benefits to the civilian sector from French defense contracts were "small." Commenting on the report, the defense analyst of the newspaper *Le Monde* wrote:

Military needs are highly specific and do not automatically lead to civilian industrial benefits, as, for example, is demonstrated by the total absence of civilian fallout of defense funds spent on the nuclear submarine program.[15]

West Germany, the European nation with the most successful postwar industrial record, has no significant defense industry. A recent white paper by the defense ministry stated bluntly that "the Federal Republic does not have a defense industry." In truth, West Germany has a small defense industry, one that traditionally has worked in collaboration with other European countries. The pernicious economic effects of even a small defense industry recently has led Germany to consider a more vigorous arms export program (Leopard tanks for Saudi Arabia) to help amortize the costs of weapons development.

Collaboration may diminish the economic ills of defense spending, but it does not eliminate them. Bonn's most disastrous experience has been with the Tornado aircraft, developed with Britain and Italy. Budgeted in 1973 at $15 million per plane, final cost for the fighter will be about $35 million. Development of a still newer fighter, called the TKF-90 and tentatively planned by Germany, France, and Britain, is now in doubt, because Bonn has questioned its ability to pay the $5.4 billion German share of project development costs.

The Boston Study Group's report on the impact of defense costs on productivity in the United States concluded that $1 billion spent in the economy would create the following numbers of jobs:

Defense industry jobs 75,000
Construction jobs 100,000

```
Personal consumption jobs . . . . . . . . . . . . . . . . .  112,000
Health industry jobs . . . . . . . . . . . . . . . . . . . . .  138,000
Education jobs . . . . . . . . . . . . . . . . . . . . . . . . . .  187,000
```

Though these figures tell us little about the effect of the $1 billion on productivity, the report states:

> Since none of the military-employed people are producing goods and services wanted by themselves or anyone else, their own demand is inflation-producing, competing for the real goods and services produced by everyone else. In contrast, every single former employee of the military service who finds civilian work, and every new employee employed with funds formerly dedicated to the military, will be adding in some way to real goods and real services demanded by the population as a whole.[16]

It is true that the United States defense industry is a significant source of income from arms exports, but its export role is not crucial to the economy. Indeed, if foreign countries now buying arms were buying civilian rather than military planes, we would be better off. General Dynamics, the leading United States defense contractor, sells only 10 percent of its aircraft production abroad; whereas Boeing, primarily a civilian contractor, is our largest exporter and does 50 percent of its business abroad. On balance, one must conclude that the defense industry's role as a prime source of inflation probably serves to price more American products out of international markets than it is able to make up through exports.

The United States today faces economic choices just like any other nation. Times have passed when we could grind out all we wanted in guns and butter and still hold inflation to 4 percent. The price we pay today in the failure to make critical choices is a falling standard of living. Our rising deficits, debts, and imbalances are only a means of passing the problem on to future generations. Though security remains as important as ever, the quest for theoretical invulnerability in a nuclear age when no such thing can exist leads us down a path filled with perils *at least* as dangerous as the hypothetical threat of a Soviet missile attack. These perils are called insolvency, no-growth, falling productivity, unemployment, foreign dependence, social discontent, crime, urban decay. One of the few American elected officials who has recognized the problem is Representative Les Aspin of Wisconsin. In a 1981 study Rep. Aspin concluded:

> It is nothing short of insane, not to mention economic suicide, for the United States to take upon itself an even greater share of the western burden while Japan and to a lesser extent Europe pump their capital into industries that are starved in the United States because of the defense umbrella.[17]

One reason why extravagant new defense expenditure today presents problems it did not a decade or two ago is that, as we have seen, we live in a different sort of economy today, one characterized by endemic high inflation, low productivity, and slow or no growth. America lacks the extra resources and idle capacity it used to have. As economist Emma Rothschild has noted:

> . . . the military boom of 1981 is likely to bring all the problems of precious expansions with few of their benefits. The two periods of greatest military expansion were both times of rapidly accelerating inflation. Thus the Korean war boom began in 1950, when inflation was one percent; in 1951 inflation was over eight percent. The Vietnam-war related military boom began in 1966 when inflation was less than three percent; since then, inflation has averaged six percent per year.[18]

If the defense budget is on the rise today following a post-Vietnam war decline, it is directly related to the evidence that the Soviet Union is increasing its military expenditures. But before examining the controversy over just how much Russia does spend on its military machine, one thing should be made clear: It is a misconception to think that the Soviet Union has been increasing its military budget in absolute terms. The CIA, the main source of statistics on Soviet military spending, does not claim that Moscow has increased defense spending absolutely. The relative rise in Soviet defense spending, like the relative rise in British defense spending, is not caused by more being spent on defense, but by a falling gross national product. (See Table 2.)

TABLE 2

Defense Expenditure

(as percentage of GNP)

	1975	1976	1977	1978	1979
Britain	4.9	5.2	5.0	4.7	4.9
France	3.9	3.7	3.2	3.3	3.9
Italy	2.6	2.5	2.6	2.4	2.4
Netherlands	3.6	3.3	3.6	3.3	3.4
West Germany	3.7	3.5	3.4	3.4	3.3
United States	5.9	5.4	5.2	5.0	5.2
(Soviet Union)	(11–13%)		(12–14%)		

Source: IISS, *The Military Balance, 1979–1980, 1980–1981*

States the CIA:

Defense spending probably accounted for 11 to 13 percent of Soviet GNP between 1965 and 1978, a roughly constant share over this period because defense and the economy were growing at about the same rate. More recently, though defense spending continued to increase at about the same rate as in the past, Soviet economic growth declined to its lowest rate since World War II. Thus, by 1979, the share of Soviet GNP devoted to the military probably increased by about one percentage point, to 12 to 14 percent.[19]

This sober assessment is hardly consistent with the charges of a "massive Soviet arms buildup" that accompanied the arrival of the Reagan Administration into office. The difference between Soviet and American behavior during the recession years of the 1970s was that the Russians kept defense spending relatively constant, while the United States allowed its to fall. Ours, however, was falling from the abnormal highs of the Vietnam war to levels consistent with past peacetime spending levels. The present planned increases would take defense spending back to Vietnam war levels, 7 to 8 percent of GNP.

Several criticisms, however, have been leveled at the CIA for its calculations. One is that it overestimates by at least 10 percent the

Soviet GNP. A compendium of papers done for a Joint Economic Committee of the Congress concluded that the Soviet GNP should be rated at no more than half ours.[20] Another analysis, done by a Soviet emigre-economist, estimated that the Soviets produce "at best one-third of what America produces and more likely one-fourth."[21] These independent analyses, if correct, suggest one of two possible conclusions: that the CIA is equally off in its estimate of Soviet defense spending or that Soviet defense spending actually pinches the Soviet economy more than we think, and thus its willingness to discuss arms control may be sincere.

The more frequent criticism of the CIA's calculations comes not on a faulty estimation of the Soviet GNP, but on the CIA's method of computing Soviet defense costs. That method consists of counting up all Soviet men and equipment and calculating how much it would cost the United States to duplicate them in dollars. This method, which the CIA claims is the best method for coming up with any meaningful economic comparisons, is alleged by critics to exaggerate Soviet spending by ignoring the differences in our two economies. In particular, the critics believe that superior American technology and productivity (yes!) is left out of the equation, as well as distortions caused by exchange-rate differentials.

The debate over how much the Soviet Union spends on defense might be dismissed as the harmless musings of stratego-academicians if on its outcome did not depend billions of American tax dollars. Yet if one thing is clear from the evidence, it is that trying to put a price tag on the value of the Soviet armed forces is a totally blind alley. The so-called Team B CIA estimate of Soviet defense spending produced in 1976 by a group headed by Richard Pipes of Harvard, Paul Nitze, former deputy secretary of defense, and William Van Cleave, a conservative political scientist from Los Angeles, doubled the estimate of Soviet defense spending from 6 to 7 percent to 12 to 14 percent and became the intellectual rationale for the Reagan defense budget. Yet as former CIA analyst Arthur Macy Cox has pointed out, the doubling did not mean that Moscow suddenly was spending twice as much, simply that "the Soviet defense industries are far less efficient than formerly believed."[22] In other words, it simply takes the Soviets more man-hours than we had thought to produce the same amount of goods.

The most sensible approach has been adopted by the London-based International Institute of Strategic Studies (IISS), which states categorically that, "no single figure for Soviet defense expenditure can be given, since precision is not possible on the basis of present knowledge."[23] This unfortunately does not help the American taxpayer. The IISS, like most military men, prefers to evaluate Soviet and American military capabilities not by how much they allegedly cost but by comparisons of men and equipment. Using this approach, the IISS concludes in its 1980 military balance that the overall balance between NATO forces, on one hand, and those of the Warsaw Pact, on the other, "is still such as to make military aggression appear unattractive."[24]

The Boston Study Group reached an even more sanguine conclusion:

Despite the larger size of the Soviet Army and the larger numbers of Soviet strategic missiles, the Soviet military establishment must still be ranked as second to that of the United States.[25]

Past experience suggests that it is futile to try to head off defense binges once the momentum has gathered. Just as the National Security Council's 1950 paper NSC-68 provided fuel for the arms race (and the hydrogen bomb) by stating that the Soviet Union "seeks to impose its absolute authority over the rest of the world," just as the Gaither report a decade later warned (falsely) of a growing "missile gap" and spurred development of the multiple-headed nuclear missile, the CIA computations will lead to defense increases today. The difference in 1980, however, is that there are restraints on the economy which did not exist a decade ago, much less two. Development costs of the hydrogen bomb and first MIRVed missiles did not exceed a few billion dollars. The MX land-based missile, which would be obsolete before its completion, is rated today at between $34 billion (the Defense Department's estimate, which must automatically be doubled), $60 billion (the General Accounting Office), and $100 billion (defense specialist

Herbert Scoville, Jr.). Air-launched MXs would cost as much. Given the scale of such costs, alternative ways must be found of achieving equal security.

The most obvious way is arms control. Defense parity can be as easily maintained at present or reduced force levels as at increased ones. The principal result of the SALT I treaty was to save both us and the Russians the incalculable costs of producing antiballistic missile systems to defend our vast countries. The SALT II treaty, had it been ratified by the Senate, would have put fixed limits on the numbers of missiles, heavy missiles, and MIRVed missiles the Soviet Union and United States could deploy. It is interesting to note that the same individuals responsible for producing the 1976 "Team B" report, Nitze, Pipes, and Van Cleave, led the fight against SALT II ratification.

Another sound economic way of dealing with increased defense expenditure would be to make Americans pay its real cost. This could be accomplished through a policy of tax increases, forced savings (through even higher interest rates), and a reduction in the standard of living. Such policy would represent a clear public choice, one that did not hide behind demagogic pronouncements that we can have more defense and pay less for it. It would cease to duck the problem of the draft. The funds made available should be spent on manpower and war-fighting equipment, not on useless missiles in desert silos, serving what one European called the "paranoid scenario" of the MX.[26]

There is yet a third way to deal with the economic aspects of defense: oblige our allies to pay more than they do, that is, bring their expenditures up to 5 percent of GNP so that ours can remain at that level. Successive administrations have tried this. Their error has been to go about it in the wrong way—by suggesting joint increases in spending. It is not through joint efforts that Europe and Japan will spend more. On the contrary, once they see that we will spend more, they will spend less. It is only by leaving them more on their own that they will spend more.

Such policy would be difficult to implement. The allies naturally are reluctant to transfer more of their resources to the nonproductive military sector. But it is sound policy for America and would lead to no diminution of our own security. It would have the added advantage over the arms control option of not allowing the Soviet Union to increase its own abysmally low productivity by transferring more of its resources to the productive civilian sector.

It would be difficult policy, primarily because our allies understand the economic advantage they now hold over us. As one European has explained it:

Power is expensive. The European criticism of the United States is to no longer accept the constraints that political power, that is a world role, place on internal development. The Europeans could become less dependent on the United States if they accepted the price of a European defense system, *which would be a considerable reduction in their standard of living* [my italics].[27]

Short of persuading them to spend more, we could at least oblige them to spend better. It is nothing short of ridiculous for the United States to encourage the British to build the $10 billion Trident submarine (more likely to be $20 billion) at the cost of cutbacks in their Navy and of British forces in West Germany. It is inconceivable that a handful of British submarines assigned to NATO could be of any use either for British or NATO defense, but one can conceive of considerable possibilities for British men and surface ships in coming years. If the British intend to remain a nuclear power, they would be better off buying cheaper Cruise missiles and putting what they save into conventional forces.

Notes for Chapter 5

1. Robert Tucker, "American Power and the Persian Gulf," *Commentary*, November 1980, pp. 28–29.

2. Robert Tucker, *ibid*, pp. 28–29.

3. *Strategic Survey*, IISS, 1980–1981, London, p. 19.

4. Ian Davidson, *Financial Times*, January 20, 1981, p. 17.

5. Alistair Horne, *A Savage War of Peace* (Middlesex, UK: Penguin Books, 1978), p. 14.

6. OECD, *Survey of the U.S. Economy*, November 1979, p. 33.

7. *Wall Street Journal*, October 28, 1980.

8. See *Le Monde* report on government energy policy, April 3, 1980.

9. *Financial Times*, January 4, 1980.

10. Robert Stobaugh and Daniel Yergin, Eds., *Energy Future: Report of the Energy Project at the Harvard Business School* (New York: Random House, 1979), p. 55.

11. *New York Times*, December 28, 1980, p. E13.

12. The statistics come from General Kelley's Congressional testimony and private conversations.

13. Seymour Melman, *The Permanent War Economy*, (New York: Simon and Schuster, 1974), p. 11.

14. Wassily Leontief, *Washington Post*, April 25, 1981, p. 8.

15. Jacques Isnard, "The Debate Still Open on Economic 'Fallout'," *Le Monde*, February 19, 1981, pp. 21–22.

16. The Boston Study Group, *The Price of Defense*, (New York: New York Times Books, 1979), pp. 296–297.

17. Les Aspin, "Aspin Hits Burden of Defending Allies," *Washington Post*, April 27, 1981, p. 5.

18. Emma Rothschild, "Reagan and the Real America," *New York Review of Books*, February 5, 1981, p. 5.

19. Testimony of Robert Huffstutler, Director, Office of Strategic Research, CIA, before House Committee on Intelligence, published as "CIA Estimates of Soviet Defense Spending," U.S. Government Printing Office, 1980, p. 7.

20. "Soviet Economy in a Time of Change," U.S. Government Printing Office, Washington, 1979.

21. Igor Birman, "The Way to Slow the Arms Race," *Washington Post*, October 27, 1980.

22. Sources for this discussion are infinite. One should see particularly, "CIA Estimates of Soviet Defense Spending," *Ibid.*; W. T. Lee, *The Estimation of Soviet Defense Expenditures, 1955–1975: An Unconventional Approach;* Abraham Becker, "The Meaning and Measure of Soviet Military Expenditure," *Soviet Economy in a Time of Change, op. cit.;* and Arthur Macy Cox, "The CIA's Tragic Error," *New York Review of Books*, November 6, 1980.

23. The International Institute for Strategic Studies, *Military Balance, 1979–1980*, p. 11.

24. *Ibid.*, p. 115.

25. Boston Study Group, *The Price of Defense*, p. 36.

26. Ian Davidson, "Nagging Doubts About U.S. Nuclear Policy," *Financial Times,* May 18, 1981, p. 17.

27. Alfred Grosser, *Les Occidentaux: Les Pays d'Europe et Les États-Unis Depuis La Guerre* (Paris: Fayard Publishing Company, 1978), p. 421.

CHAPTER 6

The New Risorgimento

"What do they know of England who only England know?"
RUDYARD KIPLING, "Recessional"

EUROPE TODAY is being stretched in opposing directions—toward unity, but toward fragmentation as well, a throwback to the regionalism of another age, a Europe not of states but of provinces. Defended semiseriously by men such as C. Northcoat Parkinson, who would divide Western Europe's dozen principal nations into thirty autonomous provinces, the movement is more serious in the hands of the separatists of the Basque country and Catalonia in Spain, Brittany and Corsica in France, Scotland and Wales in Britain, and South Tyrol in Italy. In these places we find men leading somber movements demanding more local power, but lacking consensus on means and ends to attain it. Is it to be independence, autonomy, or merely more regional power? Is it to be a peaceful conflict with a few token bombs as in Brittany or a terrorist fight to the death as in the Basque country? And what of the political terrorists, principally in Italy, Europe's latter-day nihilists, whose goal is not devolution of the state, but its dismemberment?

Social and cultural as well as political forces are at work. Having lived through an age of national unity in the nineteenth century, Europeans, like Americans, are searching today for cultural and ethnic roots threatened by the national identity. With the exception of the Basques, however, that unique aboriginal race spreading across the Iberian neck, Europe's autonomists are more demonstrative than deadly. For most it is a matter of winning back local rights lost along the way to national unity. In Brittany, for example, only a handful of Brez Atao diehards believe in the creation of an independent Breton state. It is the same in South Tyrol, in the Savoy, and in Corsica. Most regionalists would be satisfied with more cultural autonomy—the right to teach the local language again in the schools, to give children or streets special regional names, to have more telecasts and broadcasts in their own language.

The idea that is common both to regionalism and European unity, as French sociologist Guy Herand has noted, is federalism.[1] The smaller nations and ethnic groups especially, most often those living along the belt of the Rhine, seek ties both closer and broader than purely national ones, which are seen as restrictive. In Belgium, for example, two separate peoples, Walloons and Flemings, grow apart from each other even as both strive for European union. Following a century of trying to make the Belgian pot melt, today the two peoples have settled for separate but equal rights, bound politically into a single state, but separated socially and culturally. As a Fleming once told the author: "It is not that my son would not marry a Walloon if he fell in love, but that the chances of his meeting one to fall in love are small."

If cultural Balkanization is consistent with European unity, it is because of the growing awareness that in a world of Americans, Arabs, Soviets, Chinese, and Africans, there are Europeans as well. In an earlier age, when the world was Eurocentric, Europeans could allow themselves the luxury of fighting. Hobbes wrote that Europe's natural state was war, or at least so it was in his seventeenth century. Today, with the individual states too small to count alone, with the world no longer run from Europe, it is band together or drift into insignificance.

Europe today is experiencing what Italy did at the *risorgimento*. Italy did not naturally fuse as did England or even France. Italy was an example of what writer Guido Piovene called "negative unity," the achievement of union not through passionate desire for it or even the "manifest destiny" of American unification. Italian union was defensive, the least bad solution. Surrounded by the Austrian and second French empires, Italy could not afford to remain a collection of weak kingdoms and duchies defended by private *condotierri*. To survive, it was unify or perish. Europe's *Drang nach Einheit* today is no more built of the love Frenchmen have for Germans than Italy's *risorgimento* was composed of an affection between Sicilians and Piedmontese. The guiding principle, now as then, might well be found in Talleyrand's maxim: *"il ne faut pas mêler le coeur aux affaires."*

Assailed but refractory between the forces of regionalism and unity is the nation-state, conceding little but obliged to make constant adjustments that whittle down its central authority. It is not that the nation-state is threatened. It will survive as the most efficient if not most inspiring of political units. But its powers are being diluted in the separate waters of regional autonomy and European unity. Thus we see France, the nation-state *par excellence,* increasingly seeking European or regional solutions to French problems. France does not concede powers to the EEC but acts within it to increase French power. By the same token, Paris increasingly is obliged to delegate power to regional bodies and officials, reducing the power of the *préfet* (descendant of the Roman consul), the centrally appointed official sent into the provinces to rule. Under its Socialist government France is striving to end the prefectoral system.

In an age of moribund ideology, the idea "Europe" has become a source of inspiration, something to take the place of earlier discredited values. As Crozier puts it, "in thirty years, the Europeans have changed to an astonishing degree, more than anybody would ever have imagined." [2] The success of the experiment has infected the nations on Europe's fringes—Portugal, Spain, Greece, Turkey, Yugoslavia—each today seeking in some fashion entry into the club and identity in the new "Europeanness." Perhaps the germ will even spread to Europe's island, England, still finding it difficult to give up an historically self-centered identity.

It was sufficient for a former French president to suggest that Spain had not evolved enough to join the EEC for a crisis to be touched off in Franco-Spanish relations, something that a century ago would have brought out the gunboats. A "wave of anti-French feeling"[3] swept across Spain, reported one newspaper, after Giscard d'Estaing's unexpected rebuff. The French had kept Spain out under Franco, but now Franco was gone. The new passion for being European is understandable enough. The nations have grown together economically and will do so politically. West Germany's recent call for a new European "treaty of union" is but one example.

The arrival of democracy coincides with the demise of ideology. The great political dogmas of Europe are dead, replaced by fluid doctrines of social democracy, liberalism, and centrism. The political debates no longer are over Marxism versus fascism—the Reds and the Blacks—but over Keynesianism versus monetarism, demand management versus pay policies, free enterprise versus social welfare. Socialism has turned into social democracy, which in countries such as West Germany and Britain hardly is distinguishable from liberalism, itself fluid enough to flow from right to left and back again. Fascism inspires nobody but a few marginal neurotics. Communism is a fading force everywhere but Italy, where it may have peaked and in any case resembles socialism more than communism.

Eurocommunism, stillborn in the 1970s, was an attempt by several European Communist parties to win power by demonstrating they had become nonrevolutionary, more European than Communist, more democratic than Bolshevist. Though the three principal members—the parties of Italy, France and Spain—had been at odds for decades, they banded together in 1976 in an attempt to show that Europe's economic and social woes transcended national boundaries and demanded common solutions. They believed a demonstration of "international solidarity" (a phrase preferred to the more antiquated "international proletarianism") would help each party end its years in political isolation. They believed that with the renaissance in the 1970s of Eurosocialism, Communists, too, could take the internationalist road again, ending a decade of claiming to have converted to purely national roads to Marxism.

The Euro-Communists took advantage of the climate of East-

85

West détente in Europe in the 1970s and a temporary wave of antirightist revulsion. The revulsion took different forms in each country and should have been enough to help the Communists to power in at least one of them, at least as a junior partner in a coalition. In Italy the Communists were helped by mass defections from the Christian Democratic Party, defections prompted by the party's inability to provide effective government after two decades in power and the discovery of scandal and corruption within the government. In Spain the revulsion was directed against the remnants of fascism that lingered after Franco's death. In France as Gaullists fell from power and favor the electorate seemed ready to vote for a coalition of the left that would have included the Communists as a junior partner.

Eurocommunism failed in part because the three parties had little in common. Despite a professed common doctrine, something which should have bound them closer than Europe's nondoctrinaire parties, Euro-Communists in fact had less in common than most parties have. There is a degree of kinship within Europe's labor movement, within its social democratic parties, and within its liberal and conservative movements. With the Euro-Communists, there was neither kinship nor common analysis.

For the unevolved French Communists, with their nationalizations and centralized bureaucratic control, the free-enterprise Italian party hardly qualifies as Marxist at all; for the Italians, the French are the last of the Stalinists, a fading, anachronistic force. As for the Spanish party, both the larger parties regarded it as a poor old cousin—pitiful, decrepit, and senile. In truth, the Euro-Communists were unlucky. Nothing hurts the left more than recession, and by mid-1977, barely a year after Eurocommunism's conception, Europe had hit a recessionary trough. The Euro-Communists also suffered from the very moderation they hoped to profit by. In France, voters showed that if communism was to be no different than a social democracy or socialism, they preferred the latter. The same was true in Spain. Eventually, the Communist parties of both countries returned to traditional hard-line positions, appealing to dwindling corps of marginal discontents, with no hope of coming to power on their own.

If ideology is dying, then religion and patriotism—those other two historical wellsprings of European passion—are losing ground. Pope John Paul II's visit to France in 1980—the first by a pope since 181? when Napoleon took Pius VII captive at Fontainebleau—was no less than an attempt to save Christianity in France, where *la fille ainée de l'Église* was threatening the Church with that irresistible weapon the French ultimately turn on everything— indifference. It was not so much that the Church's eldest daughter was abandoning it for the wanton life as that she had become distracted. France, entering the age of technology, guaranteed wages, and seven-week vacations, was losing her spirituality. Catholicism in France was hardly more than Protestantism elsewhere. Nobody bothered with the sacraments. Of the population 90 percent admitted to being Catholic, but only 10 percent went to church.

A few intellectuals—Teilhard de Chardin, Maritain, Hans Küng, Roger Garaudy—tried to do for the age of technology what Descartes did for the age of reason: reconcile the old with the new. If religion could survive the *philosophes* and the revolution, it could survive computers and two-car households. The statistics showed that it was surviving—but as habit, not belief. Where would disaffection strike next? Already Italy was wavering, the Church's views on divorce and abortion discredited and its principal secular arm, the Christian Democratic Party, under attack. What of Spain and Portugal, two old parishioners in the drafty Iberian cathedral, once refuge from all temporal cruelties—sun, poverty, sickness, death? Was Iberia, poised to enter the new technological Europe, the next to fall? Where was the Church thriving, among young and old?— irony of ironies: only in Poland.

Patriotism we have dealt with. Squeezed between regional revival and European unity, patriotism, like ideology and religion, belongs to the age of *grand-père*. The success of the EEC put an end to the Continentals' former passion for killing each other, though that is not to say that it killed national pride. Unlike national pride, patriotism always was a concept in conflict with common sense. It had a negative rather than positive character, calling on the subject to see not only the virtues of his own but the defects (frequently genetic) of others. Today, European patriotism largely is confined to royal weddings, soccer games between Manchester United and Muenchen-Gladbach, and the Big Five rugby league: a classic case of sports substituting for war.

It is a new Europe we are facing today, culturally and socially as well as politically resuscitated. There was an age when Europe was torn by religious wars, centuries when it was rent by the struggle for political primacy; the first half of our own century was marked by the ideological clashes of the Reds and the Blacks; the latter half of the twentieth century has been distinguished by the growth of unity and consensus. This is not always perceived in America, which prefers, by habit, to focus on what is not working in Europe rather than what is. Religion, patriotism, and ideology, the fuel that drove those earlier Europes, have been replaced by motivations and drives centered on problems of society, economic development, culture, and, as we have seen, unity.

What we are witnessing today within the Atlantic structure is not only a diverging political analysis, but a diverging system of values. One should not minimize the importance of this divergence. For decades, even centuries, Americans and Europeans have assumed they held certain fundamental values in common. This communality of view would from time to time be drowned in the miasma of political vicissitude, but it always resurfaced. We held like views on the balance between the individual and the state, freedom on one hand and law and order on the other. We shared a common Western view of man as free and equal, government as benign and just, society as liberal and progressive.

In the immediate postwar period it was believed that Western Europe would be drawn ever closer to the American view of the balance between the individual and the state; as the Communist threat rose across Europe, it was assumed that Western Europe would be drawn ever closer to the American model, away from the collectivist, socialist one. From Tocqueville on (if not before), Europe had looked to America. The socialist appeal in Western Europe, even in the best of times, was a minority appeal. The majority of West Europeans, like the majority of Americans, could not stomach the idea of loss of freedom, even the erosion of freedom. Perhaps, on the whole, the European majority was slightly more interventionist than the American majority, slightly more inclined to governmental paternalism, but not so much as to speak of fundamentally diverging values.

The view from Europe today, however, is that the United States has entered a period of imbalance. To use the French phrase from cycling, we have "lost the pedals." In the chapters up to now we have traced this theme as it extends through politics, economics, and foreign relations. We must now examine it as a cultural phenomenon. To examine it is in no way to accept it. One could as easily set down a balance sheet of what is wrong in Europe today. But that is not the intent here. The intent here is to examine the reasons why the United States lost the lead it held not so long ago in many areas of human affairs and to examine the reasons why Western Europe, on its way a decade and a half ago to becoming an America, *bis* (which, after all, *was* the American challenge) has begun to go its own way.

Just as the United States dominated Europe politically and economically after the war, we dominated culturally as well. Our movies, literature, theater, music, television, and taste were everywhere. Europeans subscribed to the Paris *Herald Tribune,* wore jeans and khaki, read Art Buchwald (who lived in Paris), discovered *le jazz hot,* studied Faulkner and Hemingway, started Bogart and Jerry Lewis cults, produced Edward Albee (before he was produced in America), watched "Bonanza" and "I Love Lucy" on television. It was the time of Coca-Cola, hamburgers, and chewing gum (all still going strong). They envied us and copied us. To be an American in Europe as late as the early 1960s was an ego-satisfying experience. One found nothing of the phenomenon one finds in Europe today, where McDonald's hamburgers, in order to sell, must advertise that the product includes "no ingredients made in America."

Europe was striving to adopt our systems and our methods. By the scores Europeans came to study in American schools (particularly business schools) and work for our companies. During this period, English became the *lingua franca* of Western Europe. Some Europeans made fortunes deliberately copying American originals. The French newsmagazine *l'Express* was patterned after *Newsweek* and started after its founder spent months in New York studying *Newsweek's* operations. Anybody who looks at a cover of *Der Spiegel* recognizes its debt to *Time*.

The European identity in the postwar period was shattered, laid over successively with guilt and inferiority complexes toward the United States. The guilt grew out of the spotty European pasts—war, destruction, genocide, occupation, collaboration. It touched both the ideological right and left. If fascism lay forever discredited by its record alone, communism was not much better. What German could forget the German Communists' refusal to support the socialists and bar the way to Hitler in the 1930s? What Frenchman would forget the French party's support of the Soviet Union in 1939–1940, even after Stalin had entered into alliance with Hitler—who was at war with France? It took the Europeans long postwar years to bury those memories, and during the years of forgetting America was the model. We had come to Europe twice in the century to end their wars. With Marshall Plan reconstruction to former enemies, we showed that our magnanimity equaled our generosity.

At some point in the 1950s Europe's guilt complex gave way to one of inferiority, even if it was, in European style, laid over with a veneer of false superiority. This was the period when Europe's lingering world ambitions faded, and the Continent's new destiny was shown to be one of division and weakness. Britain and France liquidated their empires, with the United States moving in as they retreated, into Britain's shoes in the Mediterranean and East of Suez, into French shoes in Indochina. American power seemed unlimited, and, as Servan-Schreiber eventually would note, it seemed unimaginable that anyone ever could match it.

The sands ran out in the 1960s. Off to a brilliant start with the Kennedy election, by the decade's end we were in the worst crisis of our history. The social tumult of ingesting 10 percent of the population into full citizenship; the moral alienation of half the population and most of the young people over our first "bad" war, the emotional shock of discovering that a hostile superpower was determined both to match us in an arms race and widen its global influence even to our hemisphere infected the nation. Any one of these things would have been bad enough. Together they were seen as a syndrome. In the 1970s, just as we were coming to terms with these three great problems, the oil recession and presidential scandal hit us full blast.

It was during this period that Europe lost its complexes. Instead of the saviour of other times—the nation of "Lafayette, we are here" and Omaha Beach—we suddenly were no better than they. My Lai was compared to Oradour-sûr-Glane and Lidowice. Swedish Premier Olof Palme compared President Johnson to Hitler. De Gaulle made his peace with Moscow. The Europeans began to take their distance in the 1960s, a process that continued into the 1970s. They watched our war and antiwar cultures flourish, and they recoiled. The American social and cultural turmoil spread abroad, and the antiwar movement in America became an anti-American movement in Europe. This was the period of Rudi Dutschke, the Russell Tribunal, the birth of Europe's Red Brigades.

Vietnam left its mark. The protest it engendered across Europe created its own momentum, and when Vietnam faded the anger and violence remained. In the 1970s it ceased to be directed against America and was turned against those things America stood for— our culture, wealth, power, industry, consumerism. Vietnam was a parent of European terrorism. When the parent died, terrorism in countries such as Italy and West Germany became a rejection phenomenon, resistance to the transformation of old societies to the new ways, ways that might lead Europe into new errors. It was no accident that Europe's terrorism would flourish in Germany and

Italy, the two former fascists in arms, where memories were still longest on the catastrophes of their own wars. The governments of Britain, France, and the Low Countries, the victims of the fascists, could take morally forthright stands against the Vietnam war, diffusing the revulsion of the population. For the Germans or Italians there was no such catharsis; any official moral indignation would have been unseemly.

Europe came during the 1960s to lose its formerly boundless confidence in America's institutions. If from Tocqueville on they had looked up to us, with the 1960s their views reversed. In Crozier's words, "the challenge to America today is to show that she is capable of evolution and adaptation, of learning to learn."[4] And a longtime American observer of Europe put it this way:

American political and social institutions fascinated Europeans in the 1940s and 1950s because they seemed innovative and successful, while European institutions had failed. This no longer is so. It is the European institutions that seem in better health today.[5]

Getting the government off the backs of the people is no solution to the problems confronting the United States today. It is not a solution to crime and violence, to falling cultural and educational standards, to lower ethical and moral standards, to urban decay, to growing income differential, to poverty, to social discontent or family disintegration. Getting the government off the backs of the people will not explain why the United States has entered what the sociologists call the "age of narcissism" in which all value has shifted away from the collectivity toward the individual, destroying the previous balance. As America has entered what Christopher Lasch has labeled the "culture of narcissism," we have probably lost our value as a model for good. Most other industrialized democracies are moving in the opposite direction, convinced that the only hope for successful survival, economic and social, in a rapidly changing world is through consensus and common effort. Britain, under the Conservatives, has, along with America, been the other exception to this rule, and the British have paid for it with the worst urban riots and violence in their history.

The prevailing American view that the collectivity is an intruder in the affairs of the individual is a perversion of our traditional values. Instead of a healthy and creative situation in which the individual acting in his own interests serves the interests of society (an entrepreneur), or acting for his own motives serves the collective interest (the Lone Ranger), or who at the very worst does not infringe upon society's interests (the hobo, the recluse, the sourdough), we have moved into a situation in which the individual acts in his own interests against society. David Riesman sees this cultural evolution as something isolating us not only from other societies, but from our own past:

Perhaps one way of characterizing our current destructive dedication to egocentrism is to say that we do not understand the way in which individualism of our past was tempered by social controls and voluntary associations.[6]

It is likely that any society that apotheosizes narcissism in its various forms will lose touch with societies in which group structures predominate. But this is the precise situation of the European cultures. Despite our shared traditions of democracy and liberty, European society still is group-dominated, a society in which family and historical "ligatures"[7] (to borrow German sociologist Ralf Dahrendorf's word) predominate. These group identities differ from country to country in strength, but in some form are perpetuated in each. Permanent ties exist to one's family, club, cafe, parish, union, company, village, region, and nation. As some gain or lose significance, as society mutates and evolves, others take on compensatory importance. Thus family replaces church; club or cafe replaces parish; company or union replaces village or region. At some point, perhaps, supranationality replaces nationality. But the group remains.

The narcissist, however, the "me-culturist," turns inward, away from ligatures, regarding group structures as illegal strictures on self-development. Group values represent a diminishing of self. Hedonism becomes a substitute for nihilism. The effect of this on the collectivity is devastating. Not only is society negatively diminished by a nonparticipatory member, but it is positively diminished by the narcissist-hedonist's active opposition to the ethical basis for free enterprise democracy; Daniel Bell has described it as follows:

American capitalism, as I have tried to show, has lost its traditional legitimacy, which was based on a moral system of reward rooted in the Protestant sanctification of work. It has substituted a hedonism which promises material ease and luxury.[8]

It is not much of a jump from the narcissist acting in his own interests outside of society to one operating in his own interests against society. This might be one explanation of the rise of violent crime in the United States, particularly the kind of unprovoked, gratuitous crime of America's big cities, where the victim is not only robbed, but murdered; the policeman not only disarmed, but killed. Yet too often the rising crime rate is seen not as a symptom of deeper socioeconomic malignancies, of a society creating too many "marginals," but simply as a result of inadequate resources devoted to crime enforcement. The raw crime statistics (see Table I) illustrate the unique place occupied by the United States among industrialized countries.

We have mentioned the programs and policies others have adopted to deal with the social costs of economic change. They see the problem in general as one of group, not individual, responsibility, to be solved either through state intervention or consensus forged among the principal members of society—labor, business, government, farmers. But what of the area of pure culture? What is the group role in the nourishment and preservation of a nation's culture, that is, its collective creative genius—artistic, humanistic, scientific? To turn a nation's creativity over to the hands of private enterprise, what Robert Heilbroner has called the "displacement of traditional values by commercial ones,"[9] is a curious experiment. Excellence cannot always be guaranteed to bring the highest profit margins. To make the arts primarily a profit-making enterprise; to turn higher education over to private schools; to allow television, the newest educational medium, to be controlled by advertisers, these are questionable choices. Left to marketplace standards, cultural standards and educational levels can only fall, as they have. What has happened to America's magazines, to our fiction, poetry,

TABLE 1

Homicide Rates

(crude rates per 100,000 inhabitants)

	1973	1974	1975	1976	1977
U.S.A.	9.8	10.2	10.0	9.1	9.4
Belgium	1.1	1.0	.9	.9	—
Canada	2.4	2.5	2.6	—	2.6
France	.8	.9	—	.9	—
West Germany	1.2	1.2	1.2	1.3	1.2
Greece	.8	.6	.8	.7	.6
Italy	1.2	1.1	—	—	—
Netherlands	.6	.8	.7	.8	.9
Norway	.8	.6	—	.7	.8
Spain	.3	.4	—	—	—
Switzerland	.7	1.0	.9	—	.8
England	.9	1.0	1.0	1.1	1.0

Source: *Statistical Abstract of the United States,* U.S. Dept. of Commerce: Bureau of the Census 1978, 1979, 1980

art, theater, movies? Has the government no responsibility for the decline of American culture from its dominant influence in the world a generation ago?

Recent presidential reports have shown where these choices have led us. The Carter Commission on Foreign Language and International Studies (1980) reported that only 15 percent of this nation's high school students study a foreign language today (compared with 24 percent in 1965). At the very moment we have become more involved with more foreign countries we are cutting back on the necessary tools. In 1980, the Commission reported, only 8 percent

95

of American universities require a foreign language for graduation (compared with 34 percent in 1965). We have no national standards.

Another 1980 White House report, this one entitled "Science and Engineering Education for the 1980s," concluded that most Americans were headed "toward virtual scientific and technological illiteracy." The report cited a severe shortage of mathematics and science teachers and qualified faculty members in computer science and most engineering fields at the college level. It concluded that the United States, only two decades ago the scientific and technological leader of the world, today lagged behind the Soviet Union, Japan, and Western Europe in elementary and secondary school mathematics and science programs.

These reports apparently troubled one American corporation, United Technologies, enough that it took out a newspaper advertisement bearing the following message:

A University of Chicago study shows Russian high school students are ten times better educated in math and science than American students. While Ivan and Olga are waltzing through advanced calculus, Johnny and Suzy are still stumbling over fractions. It's disgraceful that at a time so crucial to our nation, many of our students aren't even learning the basics.[10]

The causes of the American fall from excellence are varied, but who would dispute that television, if not the main actor, at least has played a leading role. The 1972 Surgeon General's Report told us of the effect of television on violent crime and warned us of its long-term effect on the attention spans of American children. As a principal medium of education, television in almost every other nation in the world is kept in public hands, not lent out to private industry. It is not believed that the profit motive, the economic "bottom line," is the best means for assuring quality.

Educational statistics show that as television viewing time increases, scholastic achievement falls. According to the Nielsen Television Index, the typical American child today spends three and one-half hours per day in front of the television set.[11] If programs were improving, we could take heart, but the evidence is, as critic Harold C. Schonberg has written, that a Gresham's law of television is in operation: "Bad programs drive out good ones."[12] In New York recently, a nine-year-old boy was surrendered by his father to police after holding up a bank with a toy gun and getting away. The boy, never a troublemaker, was a television addict. "He is constantly watching crime shows on television," said his lawyer. Before robbing the bank he had watched "Adam 12," "The Rockford Files" and "Hogan's Heroes."[13]

What hope there is seems to come from public television, and if the Europeans already have a lead on us there—as the high quality of some British Broadcasting Company programming, for example, suggests—it is because 95 percent of their television already is public. We can take little heart from the first Reagan Administration budget plan, which aimed at cutting funding for public broadcasting by close to half, from $162 million to $100 million, by 1985.

Comparing our observable cultural and sociological trends with those in other industrialized countries, we see that the United States is becoming isolated. As others move in a direction that recognizes the role of the collectivity in solving complicated modern problems, the United States is reverting to values and traditions of earlier centuries. It is a singular phenomenon, one separating us not just from other industrialized countries, but from developing ones as well. Will frontier methods work for a society moving into a post-industrial phase? Will the same educational philosophy work for a country sending 50 percent of its young people to college that worked when only 10 percent went to college? Can we treat mass communication today as we did the old land grants a century ago— selling the goods to the highest bidder? Can we abandon the social wisdom accumulated the hard way during earlier decades—the government's role in regulation that came in with Teddy Roosevelt, its role in social welfare that came in with Franklin Roosevelt, its role in social justice that was promoted under Truman, Eisenhower, Kennedy, and Johnson?

We appear to others to be a society largely unable to come to grips with these problems. We know what they are, but we stand rooted, unable to act because the system itself is designed to resist change. As other Western countries respond quickly, efficiently, collectively to their needs, we remain paralyzed by a two-centuries-old constitution and traditions more rooted in a nostalgia for pre-industrial living than anything remotely connected to the turmoil of twenty-first century living.

Occasionally, a voice is raised. Chief Justice Warren Burger spoke out on the criminal "reign of terror" sweeping across American cities, one that made crime today at least as important as "the budget of the Pentagon."[14] For Burger the solution to rising crime was more law enforcement. Even the Chief Justice of the United States did not strike for the deeper level, to understand that crime, like pain, is a symptom of organic malfunction. Why has the United States today become a nation with 124 persons out of 100,000 in prison, a 50 percent increase over 1972?[15]

So we witness the fall from grace, a nation whose days as a model have run out, beset by problems and searching for solutions in nineteenth century philosophies. We witness the gradual defection of the Europeans, our closest friends and allies, and we are able to maintain what influence we have over them because they still find some use in the $200 billion we will soon be spending per annum for their defense as well as our own. But they look to us for little else today, convinced they have gotten most of what they need from us, and for most things, can do better elsewhere or their own way.

And what of the others? If the Europeans are defecting, what of the world's other 4 billion people, who will be 7 billion by 2000 if the trends hold, the population explosion that George Ball has called "mankind's second enemy."[16] In our own hemisphere, we will see Latin America become, by 2000, a region of 600 million people, two-thirds of whom will be under 25 years. What ways must we devise to keep our influence from fading in our own hemisphere? Will gunboats be enough if the teeming and impoverished multitudes have come to reject totally American values and our way of life?

Notes for Chapter 6

1. Guy Herand, *The New Nationalism* (New York: Pergamon Press, 1979), p. 132.

2. Michel Crozier, *Le Mal Americain* (Paris: Fayard Publishing Company, 1980), p. 201.

3. *Times* (London), June 23, 1980, p. 1.

4. Crozier, *Le Mal Americain*, p. 290.

5. William Pfaff, "Reflections: Finlandization," *New Yorker*, September 7, 1980, p. 30.

6. David Riesman, "Egocentrism. Is American Character Changing?", *Encounter*, September 1980, p. 19.

7. Ralf Dahrendorf, *Life Chances* (London: Weidenfeld and Nicholson, 1980).

8. Daniel Bell, *The Cultural Contradictions of Capitalism* (New York: Basic Books, 1976), p. 84.

9. Robert L. Heilbroner, "The Demand for the Supply Side," *New York Review of Books*, June 11, 1981, p. 40.

10. *Wall Street Journal*, February 12, 1981, p. 26.

11. *New York Times*, April 20, 1980, section 12, p. 7.

12. Harold C. Schonberg, *New York Times*, December 28, 1980, p. D21.

13. *New York Times*, March 2, 1981, p. B3.

14. Warren Burger, in a speech to the American Bar Association, *New York Times*, February 9, 1981, p. 1.

15. *Christian Science Monitor*, crime report, February 19, 1981, p. 13.

16. George Ball, *Diplomacy for a Crowded World*, (Boston: Little, Brown, 1976), p. 238.

CHAPTER 7

The French and
the Germans

". . . les Francais travaillent pour vivre, les Allemands vivent pour travailler."

Adage

THE RELATIONSHIP OF FEW PEOPLES is more complex than that of the French and the Germans. Though from an historical point of view the story of the French and English is probably more significant, there is a love-hate, family quality to the Franco-German affair that makes it more interesting. The story of the French and English is essentially a politico-military story, a centuries-long struggle for domination between one country ruling the land and another ruling the sea. Rival cousins descended from distant ancestors, the French and English respected each other and preferred to leave each other alone. When one tried to move onto the other's turf, the French into the Mediterranean or the seaports of the Low Countries or the English onto the Continent, they clashed. Over the centuries they established a *modus vivendi,* a shifting stalemate that kept either from achieving permanent domination in Europe. Each became the other's nemesis.

There is more than politics and distant ancestors to the story of the French and the Germans. When Clovis, King of the German Franks swept out of the Rhine Valley in the fifth century and conquered Flanders, Gaul, Burgundy, and Aquitaine, he met and mixed with a people who were basically Latinized Celts. It was Clovis and his German successors, culminating in Charlemagne, who brought unity and Christianity to this vast area, creating a realm that extended from the Alps to the Pyrenees. European unity in those days was not such a difficult matter: there were no states, just tribes, a situation that lasted until the twelfth and thirteenth centuries.

The center of the Frankish universe was the strip of territory that remains today the heart of Europe, the lands around the Rhine, stretching from the Alps to the North Sea. Charlemagne, who remained a German despite a certain affinity for the sun and women of the south, made his capital in Aachen, which the southern Franks called Aix-la-Chapelle. Aachen today still is the heart of Europe, lying at the confluence of the German, Dutch, and Belgian borders. In Aachen today the Charlemagne Prize is annually awarded to the European who has done the most for European unity. Some recent recipients: Edward Heath, Willy Brandt, Roy Jenkins, Helmut Schmidt, Simone Veil, Emilio Colombo.

In character the French and the Germans are distinct, doubtless from that element in their blood that is different. To the northern Frankish blood was added that of Huns, Vandals, Teutons, and Slavs. To the southern Frankish blood went that of the Celts (Gauls) and Latins, with a touch of Basque and Normand. These brews, as they fermented, gave off very different tastes. The first mixture tended to be heavy, disciplined, and stern, the character of the north, where survival itself depended on organization. The Franks of the south, touched by Spain and Italy, tended to a livelier disposition, more emotional, given to free expression and independence, luxuries of the warmer climes.

These traits ought not to be exaggerated. An error of those who do not know the French is to mistake them for Latins. They have their Latin blood, but by temperament they are a mixture, except for those on the Mediterranean. Few peoples are more industrious, more serious, or more organized than the French, though in their own way, which is to conceal those qualities under a camouflage of originality and high style. In temperament they tend as much to the Frankish as to the Latin. When tested, they forget their flair and are capable of pulling together in a highly orderly way. At the geographical extremities of their countries, a Frenchman and a German don't have much in common: A Provençal does not resemble a Prussian. But in the great central band of the Continent, from where the affairs and destinies of the two are managed, the people are similar. It is to this central band that control has shifted once again. As Hans Kohn has remarked on Germany: "The center of gravity has shifted from Prussia in the northeast, westward to the Rhine where it has traditionally belonged."[1]

How different history might have been if, at the death of Charlemagne's son, Lewis the Pious, the Franks had not followed the Teutonic custom of dividing up the realm among the heirs instead of the Roman one of primogeniture. Modern Germany dates from 843, the year of the partition of Verdun, when to Charlemagne's grandson Lewis went the lands east of the Rhine and to grandson Lothar the lands south, stretching from the North Sea to the Mediterranean (a third grandson, Charles the Bald, got Aquitaine and Neustria, the Western empire).

Verdun, site of the great partition, run-of-the-mill town in the Lorraine (the name comes from Lothar), has been distinguished by history for no other reason than its location at the epicenter of this "Middle Kingdom," Europe's center band, which southern and northern Franks have struggled over for a millenium. Exactly 1027 years after the partition of Verdun, a French emperor, Napoleon III, would surrender to Bismarck's Germans less than fifty miles from Verdun. And it was in the mud of Verdun that French and German soldiers fought their murderous trench warfare for nine tragic months in 1916 at the cost of half a million lives, with no ground gained or lost.

> My soul looked down from a vague height with Death,
> As unremembering how I rose or why,
> And saw a sad land, weak with sweats of dearth,
> Gray, cratered like the moon with hollow woe,
> And pitted with great pocks and scabs of plagues.[2]

Since Richelieu Europe's wars have been fought over the lands around Verdun, often for no more than a few square miles. The struggles were of the worst kind because they were family feuds. No matter what they today call themselves—Franks, Germans,

Dutch, Swiss, Luxembourgers, Belgians, Alsatians, Lorrainers, the people of the Rhine are from the same stock.

From the seventeenth century, France lived by the axiom laid down by Richelieu at Westphalia: German weakness was French strength. German policy, on the other hand, was to gather together the dispersed German-speaking peoples into a single Reich to face the united and centralized French. Obviously in conflict, these policies led to the wars of the nineteenth and twentieth centuries, culminating in the thirty-one year struggle of 1914–1945, the bloodiest war in history. A new Europe emerged from that war, one that no longer dominated but was dominated. No longer were France and Germany rival factors in world history; no longer did French prosperity depend on German weakness; no longer were Germans obsessed with the lost lands of the Rhine, for they had lost half their country to the new empire in the East. Western Europe experienced its decline and fall during the wars of the first part of the twentieth century, a decline and fall that could be traced to the Verdun partition. Renaissance would depend on reconciliation.

Following the collapse of 1945, Europe's postwar leaders set to work building a new structure, and in 1957 the Treaty of Rome was signed, setting up the Common Market. Some had wanted more swift, dramatic surgery. Konrad Adenauer, the first German postwar leader, still is suspected by Protestant Germans of wanting to split the Catholic Rhineland away from the Protestant north, join with Catholic France,* and undo what the Verdun partition had done. Adenauer eventually became one of the fathers of modern Europe, calling not for breaking up nations but for federating them. For a while, in the early 1950s, it had looked like the visionaries— men such as Adenauer and France's Jean Monnet—might succeed in creating a European federation, but national and historical patterns proved too strong. The idea of "proclaiming" Europe, of

---

*Religion has generally been a stronger unifying force in Europe than language. An example was when the Dutch-speaking Catholic Flemish revolted against the Protestant Dutch in 1830 to join with the Catholic Walloons of Brabant, forming Belgium.

instantly constituting a United States of Europe, was utopian. It would take more time.

It had never been lost on French and German leaders that, as de Gaulle told Adenauer on his triumphal visit to Germany in 1962, the two nations "complement each other in territory, labor and spirit."[3] There was indeed something complementary about the two, something which, if ever put together, would have made a formidable combination. But the old European balance of power system had not been favorable to Franco-German complementarity. That system was best described by the English historian L. B. Namier:

> On the Continent, the game of power politics, in whatever terms it was played, normally made a neighbor into an enemy, and therefore the neighbor's neighbor on the opposite flank into an ally. Hence, the rule of odd and even numbers in international politics; if Germany was France's enemy, then Poland was France's ally, and consequently Russia the ally of Germany—numbers one and three against two and four; and even sharp ideological divisions between Germany and Russia could not prevent that rule from asserting itself in 1922 and 1939.[4]

From Bismarck until 1945 Namier's law and the agressive side of complementarity dominated Franco-German relations. Each nation saw in the other its natural rival, a nation whose national interests were in direct conflict with its own. It was only with the rise of the Soviet Union, coincident with the collapse of Germany, that Namier's odd-even system broke down, and the French and the Germans began to speculate on the positive side of their complementarity. What if German steel and French coal, German industry and French agriculture, German economy and French diplomacy, German *Ostpolitik* and French *Westpolitik*, German diligence and French imagination, (the German Army and the French Army), could be put together? Would that not make a powerful combination, a nucleus of power to offset the rising power in the East? Would not such a reconciliation, the emergence of a Western power of over 100 million persons, attract the British once and for all to the Continent? The British had been tempted before. In early 1940, as the French army reeled before the Nazi onslaught, Britain had proposed an indissoluble Franco-British union to oppose Hitler. But times were not propitious for such an historic enterprise. In the victory of 1945, new possibilities presented themselves.

De Gaulle and Adenauer laid the foundation for what their successors would achieve. De Gaulle, returning to power in 1958, had had nothing to do with the formation of the EEC, but he understood that everything depended on Franco-German reconciliation. Had the two old men remained in power, the Community might have taken on a more political character, for neither was attracted by commerce or economics. In Germany Adenauer's successors, Ludwig Erhard and Kurt-Georg Kiesinger, were men almost singularly unable to maintain the political momentum generated by Adenauer. Erhard, an economist, saw Europe in little different fashion from the merchants who founded the Hanseatic League five centuries earlier, and Kiesinger, who unlike Erhard at least had a nominal interest in geopolitics, unfortunately had been an early member of the Nazi party, something which did not give him the strongest credentials for dealing with de Gaulle.

Following Adenauer's retirement, de Gaulle gave up on both Germans and Western Europe. It was during this interim period he remarked that treaties fade as quickly as young girls and roses and began a French boycott of the European community. The great Frenchman turned his attention eastward and proposed a Europe "from the Atlantic to the Urals" to end the division he saw threatening the Continent. During 1964–1968, the semiannual Franco-German summit meetings, instigated under the 1963 friendship treaty, became mournful affairs of clinking wineglasses and speeches on cultural centers. The only personal relationship of any significance was between de Gaulle and Willy Brandt, the new German foreign minister. Brandt, whose Social Democratic Party had become the junior member in Bonn's new grand coalition government, was intrigued by de Gaulle's policy toward the Russians. De Gaulle was intrigued by Brandt's interest.

Time was running out on de Gaulle. Adenauer had been dead two years when in April 1969 de Gaulle abruptly resigned following a defeat on an irrelevant administrative referendum. His style and government had been under attack since early 1968, when a student protest movement spread across the country and, supported belatedly by the leftist labor unions, became the national revolt of May–June, 1968. De Gaulle's successor, Georges Pompidou, had as little interest in Germany as Erhard and Kiesinger had in France. The irony, however, was that Pompidou's election coincided with the election of Brandt as Chancellor. Brandt, having learned from de Gaulle, turned toward the East just as France was turning back to the West.

The real significance of Franco-German estrangement during the Pompidou-Brandt period was the effect it had on two men serving under Pompidou and Brandt, both of whom were about to be catapulted into power by unforeseen circumstances. In May 1974 Brandt was forced to resign following revelations that an East German spy was employed on his staff. He was succeeded by Helmut Schmidt. Across the Rhine, only a month before Brandt's resignation, Georges Pompidou had died, a victim of multiple melanoma. Valery Giscard d'Estaing became the third president of the Fifth French Republic.

Both Schmidt and Giscard d'Estaing later would concur that the estrangement of the Brandt-Pompidou years convinced them that Europe's future depended on the union of their two countries. Without the Franco-German locomotive, the European train did not move. Both would repeat the message incessantly during their years in power as if, by constantly hearing it, their countrymen might come to believe it. Giscard's formula, in the beginning, was somewhat bolder than Schmidt's. For the Frenchman, without a Franco-German pas de deux, there was no Europe. "The Franco-German nucleus is and will remain the nucleus of Europe." [5]

Schmidt preferred to place the relationship more in an Atlantic context. In a speech at Johns Hopkins University in 1976 he gave a formula he would repeat five years later at the Sorbonne.

The relations of the European nations among themselves and with the United States are determined by the quality of the Franco-German friendship and by the growing symbiosis of our two peoples.[6]

To his friends, Schmidt would be less solemn in his definition:

The cooperation between Giscard and me in international and foreign policy is unique. It is unique because of the friendship between us; because we both realize that it is in our interest to work closely together; and because our friendship and cooperation doesn't hurt anybody else.[7]

Schmidt was not entirely correct in stating that the Paris-Bonn axis did not hurt anybody else. In most other Western European countries it was resented. The smaller countries especially disliked the Franco-German habit of meeting privately prior to European summit meetings, for the others understood that if those two agreed, it would be tough to stop them. One of the first problems faced by the British after becoming full members of the EEC in 1974 was how to deal with the Franco-German couple. The British could have joined with the smaller countries to break up the marriage or attempted to join in, turning it into a *ménage a trois*.

Interestingly, the principal French motive in 1969 for lifting the veto on British membership had been the notion that Britain's weight joined to France would be useful in keeping Germany from becoming too strong inside the EEC. Pompidou, responsible for lifting the veto, did not believe in the Paris-Bonn partnership. He believed the Germans were on their way to becoming so crushingly predominant economically that they would come to dominate Europe politically as well. The Pompidou vision of a Paris-London axis had all of the balance-of-power motivations of earlier French policy in this century—building a Franco-British *contrepoids* to German power.

But the Europe of the 1970s was different from that of the 1930s. The pressing priority of the 1970s was not creating a *contrepoids* to German power, but to Soviet power. The new French and West German leaders understood this, and the British came to as well. Britain's record inside Europe since the mid-1970s has been one of shifting alliances, at times joining the Franco-German condominium, at times opposing it to defend Britain's unique national interests. In general, however, Britain's opposition to the Paris-Bonn axis has come over internal European affairs. In foreign affairs she has tended to add her weight to the others. Occasionally, particularly under Labor Party Foreign Secretary David Owen, she publicly spoke out against France and Germany "ganging up" on the others. Britain's record under the Conservatives in the 1980s has been one of trying to join in the Franco-German game, particularly since the election of François Mitterrand and the end of Schmidt's personal relationship with Giscard. In the view of one English newspaper, Britain can have no real influence in Europe until she cracks the "Franco-German inner circle."[8]

The election of Mitterrand as France's first Socialist President of the Fifth Republic (under previous republics, French presidents had limited political powers) put Schmidt and Giscard d'Estaing's policies to the test. Not all Frenchmen and Germans had agreed that the Paris-Bonn axis was the "happiest and most astonishing development of the postwar period"[9] or "arguably the most important development of the entire postwar period."[10] In both countries Schmidt and Giscard had encountered opposition both from nationalists who wanted no special relationships at all and internationalists who would have made the Franco-German tie no stronger than some others. In France, the fear was that Bonn was at best a fickle partner, ready to be seduced by a "new Rapallo" and turn its interest toward Eastern Europe in a new version of earlier nineteenth and twentieth century *Schaukelpolitik* that kept Germany swinging back and forth in alliance between East and West.

In Germany the fear was that another French leader might abandon Giscard's centrist pro-European policy and return either to nationalism of the left (Mitterrand) or of the right (Chirac). The problem in German eyes was not so much the Socialist Mitterrand (after all, West Germany had been ruled by Social Democrats since 1969), but that the new president would be hostage to the French Communists, with their traditional anti-German and anti-European positions (reflecting the view of Moscow). Though the left wing of the Socialist party had been critical in the past of the Paris-Bonn axis, the mainstream of the party—Mitterrand, Pierre Mauroy, Michel Rocard, Jacques Delors, Claude Cheysson, Jean-Pierre Cot—was firmly in favor of a strong EEC built on the Franco-German foundation. Claude Cheysson, the government's foreign minister, had spent nearly a decade as one of his country's two permanent representatives to the Community in Brussels.

Changes in leaders do not change national interests, and the political reality is that the Paris-Bonn relationship is rooted in sound national interest. It is as much based on economic realities as political ones. As the Hudson Institute-Europe has written, "The Franco-German inner core (of the European Community) is a true economic superpower, larger than the USSR and virtually half the size of the United States. The emergence of this new superpower is an event of major historical importance."[11] The two countries today do one-third of total foreign trade with each other and are making a second attempt at hooking their currencies together inside the European Monetary System whose ambition, ultimately, is to create a common European currency.

The Franco-German partnership is also a hedge against unforeseen international developments. With the United States and Soviet Union embarked on unpredictable political courses, the partnership offers some insurance against difficulties with either or both of the superpowers. If Atlantic relations become estranged, the French and Germans may well need their union to survive pressure from the East. In dealing with Moscow their combined voice offers a better prospect of being heard.

This does not mean that France and Germany see all foreign policy questions identically, which they do not. It means simply that their common interest is to create a European voice that can be heard and that bilateral differences since 1974 have been subordinated to that idea.

There is, however, one issue that for both countries is as fundamental as the need to create a common European voice: German reunification. Up to now, German politicians have understood that the German question could only be solved inside a general European framework and that it was not so much a question of reunification per se, for few Germans believe in that, but a general East-West European *rapprochement* that would include a rapprochement between the two Germanies as well.

In Bonn today the German word for reunification—*Wiedervereinigung*—is not used so much as simply to discuss the *Deutschefrage,* the German question. The problem of reunification is the problem of reunification *of what.* No historical Germany existed that corresponds to the existing states of East and West Germany. If it is to be East and West Germany, then why not parts of Polish Silesia as well? Or perhaps Danzig and parts of East Prussia (now belonging to the Soviet Union).

There is also the great problem (for the Germans) that nobody in Europe, East or West (or in the United States, for that matter) wants German reunification. The Germans seem to understand this, and in formulating their *Ostpolitik* always have been careful to couch it in terms of East-West détente. As presented, German policy on the *Deutschefrage* is not much different from de Gaulle's policy of a Europe from the Atlantic to the Urals, nor should it be, since Brandt learned it from de Gaulle. If the French come to oppose it, it will be at the cost of abandoning one of the pillars of Gaullist foreign policy.

The Franco-German entente raises the question whether an historical enmity between two peoples can be effaced from *en haut.* At what point, in other words, does the relationship of the countries' leaders trickle down to touch the people themselves, creating a reconciliation *en bas* as well? Both Schmidt and Giscard tried to set an example their nations would follow. Their chess games, tête-à-tête dinners in Alsace auberges, and first-naming of each other in public were gestures designed to get the people to do the same. In their policies they tried to reach young people, putting the accent on youth exchanges, increased foreign language instruction, and cultural, sports, and educational meetings. France and Germany currently are organizing joint television programming directed toward young people.

The evidence suggests the campaign is bearing fruit. Recent polls show that each country has risen higher in the other's estimation. Though national preference polls are imprecise, the trends show evolution. The French have reached number two position in the German popularity polls (behind Americans), while the Germans slowly wend their way up from their traditional spot at the bottom of French polls and now occupy fourth spot, behind Swiss, Belgians, and Americans. A poll by the West German Allensbach Group showed that although the United States still was an easy first in Germans' minds, it had slipped seven points from the previous poll. The same poll showed that the French had passed both the British and Dutch in their climb to second spot.[12]

The flaw in the Franco-German partnership in the minds of some French politicians, men such as Georges Marchais, the Communist, or Jacques Chirac, the Gaullist, is that the Germans will dominate it. The French Communists still use the German bogeyman in their election campaigning, warning voters against France's liaison with the "barons of the Ruhr" and selling France out to the "Washington-Bonn axis." The Communist line is understandable enough. Somewhat more difficult to understand are the still-paranoid fears coming from parts of the Gaullist and Socialist parties. These fears reflect the belief that German economic power gradually will take over France, subordinating French industry, commerce, and banking to purely support roles in a German-run system.

The evidence suggests the opposite. Recent studies done by the World Bank and by Chase Econometrics confirm the landmark studies produced by Hudson-Europe in the 1970s showing the greater potential of the French economy. In Hudson's first report, in 1972, it was predicted that France would pass West Germany in industrial production by 1980, something which did not happen. The World Bank and Chase studies now indicate that France's *rattrappage* will take place sometime in the 1980s. These projections are based on several favorable French trends compared with the

German: a higher French growth rate, a higher French birth rate, and greater French natural resources.

West Germany is not only one of Europe's least favorably endowed countries in natural resources, but it has the world's lowest birth rate, 9.4 births per 100,000 population. The French rate, itself low at 13.8 percent, is enough higher than the German one that France should pass West Germany in population sometime in the 1990s, shortly after it passes Germany in national output.

Despite the favorable trends, some commentators believe France never will be truly competitive with Germany because of the nature of the French economy. They use a historical argument long employed to explain France's economic backwardness relative to the Germans—even during the nineteenth century when France's population exceeded the German. The contemporary expression of this view is found in the writings of such commentators as Alfred Sauvy, Stanley Hoffmann, and Michel Crozier, who view the French economy and society as variously "blocked," "stalemated," "stalled," and in general ill-adapted to the flourishing of dynamic capitalism. Wrote Hoffmann:

The stalemate society—this halfway house between France's feudal and rural past and the dreaded industrial future, this haven for an undynamic bourgeoisie driven by acquisitiveness rather than profitability, patrimoine and property rather than market expansion, security rather than risk-taking—was a unique construction.[13]

French hostility to the German connection is rooted in this notion that *la Vieille France,* traditionalist and antiquated, cannot possibly match wits with the Prussian-led hordes of the industrial north.

Though history may justify such a viewpoint, the situation was changed somewhat by France's rapid industrial growth in the 1960s and 1970s. Under de Gaulle, who devalued the franc and kept France in the Common Market; Pompidou, conservative Auvergnat banker whose mission was to industrialize at all costs; and Giscard d'Estaing, modern financial wizard whose ambition was to catch the Germans, the folksy visage of *la Vieille France* was lifted. During the recession years of the 1970s it appeared as though France's unique system of state tentacles touching all the levers of economic and social command had some advantages—at least in terms of dealing with new problems of energy shortages and rising unemployment. Giscard d'Estaing, whose obsession with Germany may have been influenced by his birth in Germany, may in the end have been undone by tampering too much with these levers. The French have their traditions, and they are not federal ones. When things aren't working the people look to Paris, something the Socialists will discover as well.

It will take more than a few years of economic success to convince the French they are in the same league with the Germans. The French commercial and industrial inferiority complex runs deep and is entirely justified. Since at least the turn of the century France has been the economic inferior of Germany, something which played a role in France's political and military inferiority as well. French economic centralization, which dates to Colbert, Louis XIV's finance minister, worked well enough during the feudal and rural ages, but, as Hoffmann and Crozier have documented, proved woefully inadequate for the industrial age.

One of the more interesting comparisons of the two systems is still found in Max Weber's *Protestant Ethic and the Spirit of Capitalism*, though Weber was not writing just of France and Germany. Weber believed that the general structure of Protestant society was more propitious to the flourishing of capitalism than Romanesque ones. His view was that certain values inherent in the Protestant or puritan ethic—thrift, industriousness, decentralization, self-reliance—were also best suited to capitalism. He wrote:

The Catholic is quieter, having less of the acquisitive impulse; he prefers a life of the greatest possible security, even with a smaller income, to a life of risk and excitement, even though it may bring the chance of gaining honor and riches. The proverb says jokingly, "either eat or sleep well." In the present case, the Protestant prefers to eat well, the Catholic to sleep undisturbed.[14]

Though Weber was perhaps unfair to French cooking, he correctly attributed bureaucracy, centralization, waste, and inefficiency to the economies of Europe's Catholic societies. At one point he borrows a phrase from Montesquieu to describe the Protestant English who, "had progressed the farthest of all peoples of the world in three important things: in piety, in commerce and in freedom." Is it not possible, Weber asks, "that their commercial superiority and their adaptation to free political institutions are connected in some way with that record of piety which Montesquieu ascribes to them?"[15]

The evidence until recently seemed to support Weber's thesis. Certainly the great Protestant societies of Europe, in particular England, Germany, and the Netherlands, became the principal industrial and trading centers. France, Italy, Spain, the closed Catholic nations of Europe, lagged behind, as did Russia, which prior to 1917 was dominated by the Orthodox Church. Weber's work had a profound influence in Europe, in some ways comparable to the influence of Marx. Like Marx his influence was limited to certain countries. Published in the original German in 1904, Weber was not translated into French until 1964. For sixty years the French had to labor on in ignorance of his conclusion that it was the failure of the Reformation that kept them from matching the German economic performance.

Despite the delay, Weber came to be known in France in the 1970s through Michel Crozier's *Société Bloquée,* which borrowed from Weber. Crozier's work had a strong influence on French politicians of the day, particularly Jacques Chaban-Delmas, prime minister under Pompidou, and Jacques Delors, Chaban's principal advisor. Their program for a "new society" aimed at unblocking the "blocked" French society through a series of decentralizing administrative reforms. These reforms ultimately were blocked themselves by Pompidou, a man of deeply traditional views, but they were picked up again following Mitterrand's election by none other than Jacques Delors, who resurfaced as a leading figure in the new Socialist government.

The idea common both to Chaban-Delmas-Delors and Mitterrand-Delors was that France needed a new Reformation—not religious but economic. Delors explained it as follows:

We want a wholly integrated economy and everyone should be able to play a part in it to the full. That is why—and this is a structural reform—we are planning a broad decentralization of French society so that we get out of the habit of directing everything from Paris.[16]

The paradox of the Socialist approach and its difference from Giscard's was that though it stood for economic decentralization, it held that the state needed to control the principal economic decision-making levers in order to decentralize them. Thus, for example, France's remaining private banks had to be nationalized and all credit brought under state control before credit decentralization became possible. By the same token, France's leading multinational firms had to be under state control to ensure that they worked in the national interest. The Socialist decentralized framework was *dirigiste*. Giscard's had been laissez-faire.

Though from an American perspective the Socialist approach looked anachronistic, from the French point of view it was more comfortable. As it happens, French economic life is run by the same economic elite, whether it be the private or the public sector. It doesn't matter much in France whether a company is state-owned or not. In addition, since 80 percent of French business financing comes from the capital market, not the venture market, it made sense to the new economists to have total control over credit. Despite its plans to extend the state's role in the economy, the new government tended to minimize the effect of the planned nationalizations, claiming that even with the new takeovers, government control would not exceed 17 percent of French gross national product, a percentage already exceeded both in Italy and Britain.

The reconciliation of the French and the Germans is the symbol of European renaissance. It is an achievement that owes as much to the wisdom of American postwar policy as to the determination of the French and the Germans themselves. What we are witnessing in the common policies of the French and Germans is the fruit of seeds sowed in the 1940s and 1950s. It is the result of our treating, under the Marshall Plan, of victor and vanquished alike; of our support and encouragement of the EEC; of our political and military aid that allowed the Europeans to recover economically; of our technology which allowed them to modernize; of our business and industrial methods which they learned and adapted to their own ends; of our (tepid) support for their East European policies, which lowered the level of European tension and helped free them from domination or dependence.

The price we paid was the emancipation of Europe. Those who criticize this process would have preferred to keep the Europeans divided and dependent. The strength of the Atlantic partnership always lay in European weakness and insecurity. It is doubtful, however, whether we would have had any more success in blocking postwar European development than we had stopping the rise of regional power everywhere. As one commentator has put it, "future historians will be stunned by the inability of contemporary American politicians to discuss frankly just how abnormal the period of great American superiority was."[17]

It was not only abnormal, but exceedingly costly. Though we may all justifiably lament the rise of an odiously repressive state such as the Soviet Union to a position of power, we should not be too inconsolable about the rise of the Europeans, our friends and allies, to a position of equality and responsibility. As George Kennan has put it:

We were not fitted, either institutionally or temperamentally, to be an imperial power in the grand manner, and particularly not one holding the great peoples of Western Europe indefinitely in some sort of paternal tutelage.[18]

Notes for Chapter 7

1. Hans Kohn, Introduction to James Bryce's *The Holy Roman Empire* (New York: Schocken Books, 1961), p. 36.

2. From a poem by Wilfred Owen, "The Show," in Oscar Williams' *Immortal Poems of the English Language,* (New York: Pocket Books, 1952).

3. French Foreign Ministry, *Major Addresses, Statements and Press Conferences of General de Gaulle,* 1964.

4. L. B. Namier, *Vanished Supremacies* (London: Hamish Manilton, 1958), p. 170.

5. See, most recently, the press conference of January 28, 1981, in *Le Monde,* February 7, 1981, p. 4.

6. Helmut Schmidt, from a recent speech at the Sorbonne, February 6, 1981; *Le Monde,* February 7, 1981, p. 4.

7. Quoted in Kurt Becker, *Die Zeit,* July 11, 1980, p. 8.

8. "Europe and the Atlantic," *Times* (London), March 7, 1980, p. 5.

9. Francois Seydoux, "Une Langue pour l'Europe," *Le Monde,* March 15, 1980, p. 2.

10. *Sunday Times* (London), March 30, 1980, p. 16.

11. James O. Goldsborough, "The Franco-German Entente," *Foreign Affairs,* Spring 1976, p. 501.

12. *The Week in Germany,* March 7, 1980, p. 5.

13. Stanley Hoffmann, *Decline or Renewal* (New York: Viking Press, 1974), p. 449.

14. Max Weber, *The Protestant Ethic and the Spirit of Capitalism* (New York: Scribner's, 1958), p. 41.

15. *Ibid.,* p. 45.

16. Jacques Delors, Interview in *l'Usine Nouvelle,* May 14, 1981.

17. Robert Kaiser, "U.S.-Soviet Relations," *Foreign Affairs,* Vol. 59, No. 3, p. 505.

18. George F. Kennan, *Memoirs* (Boston: Little, Brown, 1967), p. 490.

CHAPTER 8

Englanditis

All over the world each nation's
    the same.
They've simply no notion of playing
    the game.
They argue with umpires, they cheer
    when they've won,
And practice beforehand, which ruins
    the fun.
                  (chorus)

The English, the English, the English
    are the best.
I wouldn't give a tuppence for all of
    the rest.
                  (refrain)
        Flanders and Swann,
   "Song of Patriotic Prejudice"

ENGLANDITIS is a classier word for what used to be called the "English sickness," the qualities of which curiously resemble those associated with mononucleosis. Mononucleosis is an affliction caused by a virus of unidentifiable strain whose symptoms include fatigue, fever, loss of will, irregular behavior, and fits of churlishness. It requires treatment but not hospitalization; convalescence is long and tiresome, usually putting the patient so far behind his contemporaries that he has little hope of catching up. However easy it may be to identify the symptoms of Englanditis, doctors have had no success at all isolating the virus. Scores of attempts have been made, some dating back a century. We know it is of political, economic, and sociological origin, but that is too general to be of help, making the cure difficult.

Britain has, in the space of half a century, fallen from first place among industrial nations to a place somewhere between Spain and East Germany on the list of countries ranked by per capita income.

In other countries such decline and fall would have led to revolution or at least a coup d'état, but Britain does not do things that way. Instead, British government has oscillated between Conservatives and Laborites, giving each party its go at finding the cure. Neither has succeeded noticeably better than the other, and each blames the other for undoing its work during the alternation. Both parties seem convinced that the malady's cause is economic, and so believing bring with them into office each time a satchel of economic "cures." As the 1980s got underway, the Conservatives were having their innings trying out a Friedmanite treatment of monetary control, deregulation, reduced public expenditure, and unemployment. The cure was severe enough that, during the summer of 1981, Britain's industrial cities erupted in an orgy of violence and rioting, which the government itself conceded was motivated by its draconian economic policies.

Though consensus between political parties with names as provocatively different as Conservatives and Laborites is no easy matter, the two did manage to agree on one policy over the course of the past quarter century: Britain had to join Europe. It was not an easy decision, and it came late, some would say too late. Strong minorities in each party opposed the European move during difficult years of negotiation in the 1970s, but the majorities prevailed. When in June 1976 the British people were given their first-ever national referendum, the solid vote to support membership was a surprise to all. Though polls had shown the people cold to an alliance with a group of Continentals they were more used to fighting than joining, voters backed membership in the referendum two to one. It was a stunning victory for the British "Europeans." But the war was not won.

Joining the EEC was an act of wrenching decisiveness for the British. It meant abandoning a history of turning their backs on the Continent, no longer facing the Empire, facing America. In his memoirs de Gaulle recalls a phrase of Churchill during the war: forced to choose between the Continent and the open seas, Britain would always choose the seas. That notion later played a strong role in Gaullist policy throughout the General's years in office, as he strove to make sure Britain remained on the open seas. Churchill saw Britain as co-leader of the Anglo-American alliance, as leader of the Empire, as leader of the English-speaking peoples. He did not see Britain as a leader of Europe.

Just as Churchill lost his place as Britain's leader before Europe's guns were cool, so did Britain lose its place as a world leader. As the Empire shrivelled, Dean Acheson remarked Britain had "lost an empire and not yet found a role." If the Empire was gone, so was co-leadership with the United States. Britain came out of World War II, in Henry Morganthau's words, "busted." In 1946 Lord Keynes came to Washington seeking $6 billion to help the country meet its wartime debts. Britain owed $20 billion to the United States in lend-lease payments, which were, with Keynes' help, later cancelled. There was no way the Anglo-American wartime partnership could have remained a partnership of equals. By 1947 Britain was forced to withdraw foreign aid and forces from the Eastern Mediterranean, which for a century had been a pivot in the English sphere of influence. In 1948, with the Truman Doctrine, the United States moved into the Mediterranean to replace the British.

No man deserves more blame than Churchill in the debacle of British postwar foreign policy. In a Zurich speech in 1946, while out of power, he had seen what was coming and called for a "United States of Europe" to replace the fading empire and the broken states of the ruined continent. What he did not say was that he envisaged this United States without Britain.

Continental Europe was a place to be pitied and helped but not joined and when Churchill and others urged Europeans to bury their hatchets and unite, he was not proposing that Britain should join the union—although other Europeans did not realize this.[1]

Pity is the wrong word; disdain would be better. British disdain for the Continent goes back far in history and is heard in such popular phrases as the "wogs begin at Calais." The British historically felt superior to the Continentals, even France, the only other European country which in British eyes could properly call itself a state. The Germans probably summed it up best in a saying about the difference between a Frenchman and an Englishman: "the Frenchman thinks he is superior; the Englishman knows he is." But British superiority in the postwar era, as the "Song of Patriotic Prejudice" makes so powerfully clear, was sheer illusion.

By the early 1950s, Britain's superior attitude toward the Continentals was misplaced and already affecting Britain's capacity to assess correctly what was taking place in Europe. In May 1950 French Foreign Minister Robert Schuman, an Alsatian (born when Alsace belonged to Germany), announced the Schuman Plan, the pooling of French and German coal and steel production, in a schematic sense an exchange of French coal against German steel. "It is not a coal and steel association," remarked Jean Monnet, "it is the beginning of Europe."[2] Britain, first under Labor and later under the Conservatives, elected to stay out of the Coal and Steel Community. Six years later, when the EEC itself was set up, the precedent was established, and Britain declined again.

We have already described the economic ascent of Western Europe following the formation of the EEC in 1957. There would be no such ascent for Britain. Having elected to stay outside the Community, Britain began to slip relative to the Continentals, and the doctors began to have real doubts about the patient's prospects for recovery. No one dates the decline from 1957. Most analysts agree with Hobsbawm that the British relative industrial decline goes back a century.

. . . this sudden transformation of the leading and most dynamic industrial economy into the most sluggish and conservative, in the short space of thirty or forty years (1860–1900), is the crucial question of British economic history.[3]

The beginning of the British *relative* decline probably is not too significant. Britain is, after all, the oldest industrialized nation and it was natural for the newer countries to close ground once they got started. What is important are the comparative figures before and after 1958, the first year the original six-nation Community functioned as a unit (with Britain outside). The figures show the 1958

TABLE 1

Comparison of Gross National Products

(in billions of dollars)

	1958	1980
Britain	64.8	513.9
Major EEC countries		
West Germany	58.5	822.7
France	53.9	652.4
Italy	30.3	388.6
United States	455.0	2555.4
Japan	32.0	1045.0

Source: *Basic Statistics of the Community 1968–69*, p. 24; *OECD Observer*, March 1981

British gross national product roughly 20 percent higher than the French and 10 percent higher than the West German (see Table 1). Twenty years later, the West German GNP would be half again as great as the British, while the French was a full third greater than the British. Britain's decline relative to the nations of the EEC after 1958 was precipitous.

The political mistake eventually became apparent to both parties. In July 1961 under the Conservative leadership of Harold Macmillan, Britain formally applied for membership in the Community. Negotiations began, but came to an abrupt end in January 1963, when de Gaulle vetoed the British candidacy. At a press conference January 14, 1963 de Gaulle announced:

The Common Market of the Six forms a coherent whole; they have many points in common while Britain is very different. She is scarcely an agricultural country at all and, unlike the Six, she has special political and military relations with the outside. For a long time, far from wanting to enter the Common Market, she has tried to impede its progress.[4]

Prior to the veto de Gaulle had appeared to be leaning toward British membership. Most accounts agree, and are corroborated by de Gaulle's own statements, that it was the Nassau nuclear agreement between President Kennedy and Prime Minister Macmillan in December 1962 that finally turned de Gaulle against the British. The French had believed in the possibility of France and Britain pooling their nuclear forces to form a European deterrent. The idea had come up during EEC negotiations. Instead, under the Nassau accord, the British went with the United States. "Britain transferred to the United States all the meagre nuclear forces in her possession," de Gaulle later remarked. "She could have handed them over to Europe. Well, that's a choice she made."[5]

By 1964 the Labor Party, too, had rallied to the idea of European membership, but negotiations would not get going again until 1969, following de Gaulle's resignation and the election of Georges Pompidou. Under Pompidou and British Conservative Prime Minister Edward Heath, a staunchly pro-European, negotiations were successfully concluded. Seventeen years after the EEC was established by the Treaty of Rome, Britain became a member. The date was January 1, 1974—precisely as the world recession hit.

We will come to the underlying sociopolitical causes of Englanditis in due course. But any discussion of the disease cannot ignore the proliferation of economic diagnosis over the past two decades. So comprehensive is the economic analysis that one has the feeling of understanding everything about disease in general and nothing about the particular patient. Each analysis provokes a counteranalysis. Schools spring up around each theory and attract politicians anxious to put them into practice. Because Britain is an island, imaginations are excited the world over of economists weaned on the classroom concept of an "island" economy, where constants and variables can be isolated and analyzed with all the precision of the laboratory.

Most of the relevant studies have come in the past decade and a half. Almost all were influenced by the exhaustive work of E. J. Hobsbawm who argued—like Americans would about Europe a decade later—that Britain had entered a climacteric or down side of a life cycle. Like any organism past its peak, Britain could not hope to compete with the vigor and energy of youth. Hobsbawm, an historian, was not attempting to be prescriptive. He suggested that a number of economic, technological, sociological, political, and industrial factors were at work. His work had a deeply pessimistic influence on British scholars.

Let us examine some of the economic diagnoses in a summary manner:

LACK OF ECONOMIC SIZE.   This theory was first advanced by Edward Denison of the Brookings Institution. Denison argued that the British exodus from the farm in the nineteenth century left the nation with no excess manpower to draw on in the 1950s and 1960s. Consequently, while the Continental countries shifted manpower and increased productivity, Britain stagnated.[6]

TOO FEW PRODUCERS.   This diagnosis was advanced in 1967 by two Oxford professors, Robert Bacon and Walter Eltis. They believed the cause of decline to be government policies that had allowed the working population to shift out of industry and into service professions such as banking, insurance, brokerage, tourism, law, and shipping, in which no product was produced. Thus, argued Bacon and Eltis, British productivity was destined to trail that of the more industrial nations.[7]

TOO MANY PRODUCERS.   This notion, advanced by Michael Beenstock (and others) holds that the service sector is Britain's best bet for salvation. Beenstock argues that British industry is bound to be squeezed (in the Hobsbawm sense) by the young industries of developing nations and that the highest levels of British productivity can be obtained in tertiary sectors where Britain has the widest experience. This argument has been adapted to show that Britain may now be on the upside of the climacteric.[8]

THE LABOR UNIONS.   Labor's role in the disease is cited by too many sources to give them all credit. Politically, labor excess has been the rallying cry of the Conservative Party since the early 1970s. Conservative newspapers such as the *Daily Telegraph* and commentators such as Peregrine Worsthorne do not put too fine a point on it: "Nobody ever replies [to the unions] with equal bluntness," wrote Worsthorne, "telling the workers to go and get stuffed."[9] Worsthorne's contribution to a remarkable little collection of 1977 essays called *The Future That Doesn't Work* was perhaps the most virulently critical of labor, but the same strain ran through other essays in the book, especially those by economic writers Peter Jay and Samuel Brittan. Curiously, the evidence does not bear out the thesis that labor is the chief culprit. British wages, according to EEC statistics, are the lowest in the Community (see Table 2). What's more, even with the whopping wage settlements

TABLE 2

Hourly Labor Costs in Industry [1]

(in U.S. dollars)

	1972	1975	1976	1977
West Germany	3.51	5.76	6.70	7.60
France	2.65	4.59	5.30	5.80
Italy	2.66	4.20	4.60	—
United Kingdom	2.11[2]	3.02	3.10[3]	3.20[3]

Source: *Basic Statistics of the Community,* 1979
[1] Manual and nonmanual workers in establishments with 10 and more employees
[2] 1973
[3] Manufacturing industries

of 1974–1975, British wages since 1970 have increased at a slower rate than the EEC average.[10] As for the notion that British labor is more strike prone than other labor, the statistics are mixed. The British Employment Gazette shows that in the period 1965–1974 Britain lost fewer days due to strike action than the United States, Italy, or Canada. It was the same in the five years 1975–1979. However, during both periods among EEC countries only Ireland and Italy had worse records.[11]

FALL IN PRODUCTIVITY. Analysts such as Lord Kahn, Peter Jay, and Samuel Brittan attempt to demonstrate that the *absolute* fall in British productivity since 1975 stems from the large wage settlements of the 1974–1975 and 1978–1979 periods. There would appear to be some connection. Between 1965 and 1975, British wages went up an average 6.5 percent, and the British productivity decline was only relative. From 1975–1979, however, wages increased at a rate of about 15 percent, and the fall in productivity was absolute. But wage settlements since 1975 have not been the only problem. The worldwide recession began in 1974. A study by the Brookings Institution establishes a definite connection between the rise in the price of world commodities after 1974 and Britain's particular plight over the subsequent years.[12]

GOVERNMENT SPENDING. Economist Milton Friedman long has preached that Britain's troubles stem from too much government spending. Though there may be some truth to this view, British government spending as a percentage of gross national product is about average for the EEC—roughly 40 percent.

EDUCATION AND MANAGEMENT TECHNIQUES. This is the particular theory of economist Robin Marris. "What is appalling," writes Marris, "is that a quite startlingly low proportion of British middle and upper-middle management, even as late as the middle 1960s, had had any higher education at all as compared with Germany and France, let alone the United States." And again: "I believe that what we have at work here is a kind of technological and commercial backwardness or decline. The British are always one step behind what the market is doing technically and commercially."[13]

DEMAND DEFICIENCY. This is the theory of the Cambridge Economic Group, which has a strong influence on the left wing of the Labor Party. The Cambridge thesis, simply put, is that Britain should withdraw from Europe and retreat into its island economy, closing the doors to the outside, using funds now paying for imports to stimulate domestic demand and increase domestic production. The Cambridge "fortress economy" plan would have the virtues and defects of fortresses anywhere. The fortress would be self-sufficient, cut off from the outside, and administered through severe control and regulation. The population would be safe but miserable. Such policy would bring a preposterous drop in the standard of living. As economist Brittan has remarked on the Cambridge proposals: "It would be like the man who has failed to hold down a succession of jobs and in desperation takes to the bottle."[14]

INDUSTRIAL BACKWARDNESS.   This notion was advanced in a study done by the Hudson Institute-Europe.[15] Hudson believes Britain is not investing enough in new equipment to remain competitive with other industrialized nations. Statistics do not support the claim.

LAZINESS.   One finds this notion in a wide range of articles. Daniel Bell made much of it in his study of Britain. In essence, it holds that Britain has entered a new era dominated by the notion of "the right not to work." Rather than striving to increase production, the British are concerned with how to reduce work hours. Anything that serves this goal is good, whether it be shorter hours, longer holidays, featherbedding, longer teatimes. To accept this idea is to accept that Britain has adopted a new post-industrial mentality in which the workers would rather see standards of living fall than work harder to raise them. It is a questionable point. Quality of life, in this view, rather than quantity, is what matters: pub time rather than overtime. Asks Bell: "Naturally, one does not want to deprive England of its high quality of life. The only question is: Can the British afford it?"[16]

If there is truth to the Bell thesis, one is at a loss to know whether this represents positive or negative development. Is this decline or ascent? It would certainly contradict Max Weber's views on Protestantism and the work ethic, but then Britain long has appeared the exception to Weber's analysis. The flaw in Bell's thesis is that the trend toward more leisure time is not unique to Britain and therefore cannot be the cause of Englanditis. Labor unions in various nations have taken to negotiating fringe benefits rather than wage increases in recent settlements. In France labor is striving to obtain government recognition for a *minimum* of six vacation weeks per year, plus, of course, the usual holidays. It is the same in West Germany. The trend for more leisure is present in the United States as well.

It is a particularly futile enterprise to diagnose the English disease as something related to one or another of these economic quirks. Idiosyncrasies in economic and industrial performance are found in every industrialized country, and to single Britain out as the only nation with pernicious characteristics is arbitrary. West German industry had to labor for over a decade under the burden of an appreciating currency that seriously affected the West German capacity to export. Sociologist Ralf Dahrendorf stressed in his masterly study of modern Germany that German industrial structure is fraught with imperfections, many left over from the days when German industry was still the *chasse gardée* of Prussia.[17] French industry has had to shake off a centuries-old patina of fustiness and protectionism to compete in the free trade industrial world. The Italian industrial structure is a mixture of state-run cartels (Italy has the highest percentage of nationalized industry in Western Europe) and backroom shops of a dozen workers. To argue that Britain has been attacked by a unique economic virus unlike those affecting other nations is to deny the contagious qualities of germs.

A treatment that has received particular attention has been administered lately by Margaret Thatcher and her Conservative government, elected in 1979. Mrs. Thatcher, strongly influenced by the monetarist economics of Milton Friedman, came to power pledging to cut public expenditure, reduce the money supply, and stimulate investment and productivity. Mrs. Thatcher was two years ahead of Reagan with Reaganism, and the results were not good. It used to be in the 1960s that Britons thought the nation could not put up with 500,000 unemployed without street riots. It took unemployment to reach 3 million in 1981 for the riots to begin. Despite constant official reminders that the recession had reached bottom, it continued to worsen. The only hope for the Tories was the split in the Labor Party. By 1981, even Milton Friedman, to avoid discredit, was complaining that the Tories' problem was not their monetarism, but that they had not been monetarist enough.

By mid-1981 one could find favorable, unfavorable, and mixed signs in the British economy. Favorable was that Britain, alone among major industrial countries, had become a net oil exporter, eliminating what had become for most countries the number-one economic problem; also favorable was the declining rate of inflation. Unfavorable was that at 2.9 million, British unemployment had set an historical record. A mixed sign was found in the sterling exchange rate. The pound gained strength so rapidly during the 1979–1981 period of North Sea oil development that Britain found its industry being priced out of many world markets. In 1980 alone, sterling rose 21.5 percent against the Deutschemark. The rapid rise prompted the diagnosis that Britain had been afflicted by a new disease, the "Dutch disease," whose symptoms are energy independence, strong currency, declining industrial exports, and high unemployment. Mrs. Thatcher dismissed such notions:

. . . there is a time when you are still suffering from the disease and you take the medicine and there is a time when you are suffering from both the disease and the medicine. That doesn't mean you stop the medicine; you know you have to take the medicine if you are to be cured of the disease.[18]

No one doubted Mrs. Thatcher's courage, but as her third year in office ran down, many doubted her judgment—economic and political. Daughter of a shopkeeper, Mrs. Thatcher had a shopkeeper's faith in the virtues of free enterprise, self-reliance, and laissez-faire. And she discovered that in a complicated modern economy entering a post-industrial phase it took more than a shopkeeper's virtues to run the country. The people may have been inspired by her determination and rhetoric, but they would not stand for her policies. Though Reagan Administration economists denied it, there was a lesson for America in Mrs. Thatcher's performance. Two years before Reagan, she had tried a similar experiment—getting more funds back in the hands of the people. With interest rates at 20 percent, it did not work. The people did not spend the money.

Taxation is not the cause of Englanditis. If it were, many countries with higher tax rates would be in worse shape.

The true cause of Englanditis is rooted in sociopolitical not economic failure. Perhaps it was inevitable. There is a British penchant for clinging to tradition, sticking to habit, and believing that what has worked will go on working. Few peoples are as addicted to clubby routine. British life is dominated by a daily ritual that outsiders regard as quaint and dull until they have lived there long enough to fall victim to it. As one observer has described it:

The mutual tolerance that makes the daily life in Britain so attractive to many foreigners indeed prompts an acquiescence in things as they are and a willingness to cope with imperfection rather than make a scene. This tolerance plays into the hands of those who resist change because they have something to lose from it.[19]

Insular living creates patterns altogether alien to the hum of life on the Continent. The wogs still begin at Calais. Perhaps no British politician no matter how bold or prescient could have dragged Britain back from the open seas and moored her to the Continent before demonstration had been made that the craft no longer was seaworthy. Even when the demonstration had been made, it was difficult to change course. Today, when few objective observers suggest that Britain has any future except moored to the Continent, many Britons still cannot accept that they no longer are the head of something, simply members. Though the island has no place else to go, the Continent remains alien to it. Perhaps the English Channel tunnel, when it finally is built, will change that.

As it is a trader's job to know where prices are going, it is the politician's job to know where the future lies. In doing their jobs British politicians were singularly lacking. They followed the crowd instead of leading it. Churchill had as much opportunity for postwar greatness as de Gaulle, but he did not seize it. It would have been equally easy for the French to take refuge in wispy dreams of empire, and for a while they did, but they soon came to their senses. De Gaulle, as much a nationalist and traditionalist as any Englishman, might have turned his back on Europe when he returned to power in 1958, and many thought he would. But he kept France in the Community and laid the groundwork for the modernization and industrialization of the country. De Gaulle, like Churchill, might have followed the public mood. He might have fought on in Algeria or partitioned it in typical British style and seen France drained by decades of civil war, as Britain has been in Ulster. The British lay basking in faded memories of Khyber longer than was good for them.

The result of the political mistake was that Britain continued too long in her prewar colonial patterns of exchange: exports of classical industrial manufacture, automobiles, and textiles; imports of raw materials and foodstuffs. In the early postwar period such exchange provided decent enough returns, for the prices of commodities from the colonies and former colonies were remarkably low. Sterling balances that flowed into Britain from the colonies to finance British deficits were re-invested by the British in the colonies. While the Continent went about the job of modernizing itself, the British went about the job of modernizing the Empire. But the Empire was a soft, protected, unindustrialized market, unable to provide British industry with the industrial vigor it would have gained in the dynamic free trade markets of the Continent. The longer Britain stayed outside Europe, the wider the gap opened. Britain became an imperial switching station, the nerve center for a railroad running on a different gauge from Europe. The longer she played that role, the more track she laid, the more difficult it became to change the roadbed. Later, as weeds grew up on the tracks and rural stations shut down, Britain was left with a ghost railway.

What of Britain's future in Europe? The British still feel sufficiently insular to refer to the Continent simply as "Europe," as though Britain were a part of some other place. Yet no matter how distasteful they find it dealing with eight squabbling continentals with their babble of tongues, exotic habits, and unfathomable Latin and Teutonic methodology, there is no other course. On a deeper level not always shown in polls and public statements, this is understood. Britain by every measure (though it is not readily admitted) is becoming more European daily. The British may fight to change the European system and make it more to their liking, but there can be no serious question of leaving it. The British Labor Party has not understood this at the risk of its own survival.

The split in the Labor Party and founding of a Social Democratic Party came largely over the question of EEC membership. The 1979 Labor manifesto stated that if certain conditions were not met, "the Labor Party would have to consider very seriously whether continued EEC membership was in the best interest of the British people."[20] This idea that a future Labor government might pull out of Europe caused such a rift that it appeared Britain was moving away from a fundamentally two-party system toward a more Continental style of government dominated by coalitions.

It was not Britain's economic performance within Europe that prompted hostility so much as a rising "Little England" mentality that believed Britain could successfully return to the days when she went it alone. The EEC statistics, in fact, are increasingly favorable. In 1980, for the first time since joining, Britain ran a trade surplus with the Community. The surplus—a modest $144 million—represented considerable improvement over a $7 billion trade deficit the year before. The gain reflected not only a strong improvement in oil exports, but better performance in exports of industrial goods as well. Although there was reason to believe the favorable trend would not resist the sharp rise in the price of sterling, the trade statistics, said the *Financial Times,* set off the "first signs of public optimism" about EEC membership.[21]

One ultimately must deal with the question of what is America's best interest in this changing British situation. For almost a quarter century following World War II Americans and British believed in a "special relationship," one defined not only by common language and the wartime experience, but by shared values and interests. We held to the relationship even as events began to demonstrate that our interests, at least, no longer were so common. The Suez crisis of 1956 was a turning point, but more important was the dawning awareness inside Britain after EEC formation in 1957 that it was a mistake to stay out. To rectify that mistake was to end any claim to a special relationship, though the British did not see that at the time. So long as they believed they could have both, they had, in effect, neither, for they were frozen out of Europe for fear of being America's "Trojan horse," and distrusted in America for fear of having become too European.

European political development would have taken a different course if Britain had joined in 1956 rather than 1974. Not only must we assume that European union would have come more rapidly, but it is likely Europe would have developed a unified military potential as well. The European Defense Community Treaty, rejected by the French Parliament in 1954, would have been ratified with Britain joined to it. The French, from 1950 on, had searched for ways to tie the British to Europe. A European defense force with Britain inside would have made French acceptance of German rearmament easier. But the British declined, a decision that was "decisive for the French, who lived in such fear of German hegemony on a continent from which Britain was absent."[22]

Let us not shed too many tears over the demise of the special relationship. Whatever Anglo-American value it might have had was outweighed by the damage it did to us with the others. The West Germans misunderstood it; the French manipulated it; the others resented it. It kept Europe weak, which was not in our interest. America's intention and stated policy from the Schuman Plan on was the creation of a united and strong Europe, one which could be, in President Kennedy's description, one of the "twin pillars of democracy." Our applied policy was not consistent with our stated policy. By clinging to the notion of a special relationship long after one existed, by granting the British special favor, we defeated our purpose. The real strength of Western Europe—and its real value to us—lies in the combined strength of its members.

Notes for Chapter 8

1. Peter Calvocoressi, *The British Experience* (New York: Pantheon Books, 1978), p. 218.

2. Quoted in James O. Goldsborough, "The Franco-German Entente," *Foreign Affairs,* April 1976.

3. E. J. Hobsbawm, *Industry and Empire* (London: Penguin Books, 1968), p. 178.

4. French Foreign Ministry, *Major Adresses, Statements and Press Conferences of General de Gaulle,* 1964.

5. Alexander Werth, *De Gaulle* (London: Penguin Books, 1965), p. 327.

6. Edward F. Denison, *Why Growth Rates Differ* (Washington, D.C.: The Brookings Institute, 1967).

7. Robert Bacon and Walter Eltis, *Britain's Economic Problems: Too Few Producers* (London: Macmillan, 1976).

8. Dr. Michael Beenstock, *The Causes of Slower Growth in the World Economy* (London: London Business School, 1980).

9. Peregrine Worsthorne, *The Future That Doesn't Work* (New York: Doubleday, 1977), p. 7.

10. European Community, *Basic Statistics, 1979,* pp. 141–145.

11. *Department of Employment Gazettes,* December 1975; December 1980.

12. *Britain's Economic Performance* (Washington, D.C.: Brookings Institute, 1980), pp. 36–38.

13. Robin Marris, *Is Britain Dying?* (Ithaca: Cornell University Press, 1979), p. 93.

14. Samuel Brittan, *Financial Times,* April 17, 1980, p. 19.

15. Hudson Institute-Europe, *The United Kingdom in 1980* (London: Hudson Institute, 1974).

16. Daniel Bell, "The Future That Never Was," *The Public Interest,* Spring 1978, p. 35.

17. Ralf Dahrendorf, *Society and Democracy in Germany* (New York: Norton, 1967).

18. Interview with Mrs. Thatcher in the *Times* (London), May 5, 1980, p. 6.

19. Richard E. Caves, *Britain's Economic Performance,* p. 142.

20. *The Economist,* November 17, 1979, p. 24.

21. *Financial Times,* January 19, 1981, p. 14.

22. Louis J. Halle, *The Cold War as History* (New York: Harper and Row, 1967), p. 254.

CHAPTER 9

Eastern Europe and the USSR

"I am full of sympathy for the Poles, but if we are to exist we can do nothing except root them out; the wolf cannot help having been created by God as he is, but we shoot him all the same when we can." [1]

OTTO VON BISMARCK

SOVIET LEADERS from Khrushchev on must have wondered about Stalin's decision to reconstitute Poland as a nation following the defeat of Nazi Germany in World War II. For almost two centuries the European powers had kept Poland partitioned on the grounds that, united, it was too much for any of them. For most of modern history Europe has had no Poland or, more correctly, has had three Polands—Russian, Prussian, and Austrian. When the victorious Western allies resuscitated Poland in 1919 following the defeat of Kaiser Germany and the Bolshevik revolution in Russia, it was the first time since the eighteenth century that Poland returned to Europe as a sovereign and united state. Modern Poland was destined to live a precarious existence. Attacked in 1920 by the Bolsheviks bent on regaining territory, the Poles were briefly victorious. Nineteen years later, Stalin and Hitler consummated the fourth partition, and Poland disappeared from the map again.

Victorious in 1945, Stalin had no master plan for devastated Poland. With a fifth partition ruled out, since there was nobody to partition with, the evidence suggests he regarded Poland as he did Finland, a conservative nation where Communism would never take, where it would suffice to establish a regime not hostile to Russia—even if, as in Finland, it was not Communist. Stalin made changes in Polish borders, taking back some 100,000 square miles of disputed Polish-Russian territory on the eastern frontier and compensating by giving the Poles 60,000 miles of what had been Germany, but he did not move the new Soviet boundary farther west than the 1923, British-established Curzon line, in other words took no territory to which Russians did not have at least as great legitimate claim as Poles.

The immediate fate of Poland was determined by the course of events in 1945–1947, the growing hostility between East and West and the beginning of the cold war. Though the Big Three powers had agreed in 1945 at Yalta that the future of Poland would be settled by free elections, it was clear by 1947 there would be no elections. By 1947, Western statesmen were convinced Stalin was out to take not only Poland but all of Eastern Europe. For his part, Stalin saw in the Marshall and Truman plans attempts to do what the West unsuccessfully had tried to do after World War I—drive the Bolsheviks from all of Europe. What had until 1947 been still unresolved lines of political demarcation began to congeal into fixed division.

After 1947 it would be left to Poles and Russians, not the West, to determine Poland's future. But the new Poland, though it became Communist, had an advantage over previous Polands: the nation was entire again, with a population close to 30 million. For either Bismarck or Stalin it would take a lot of digging to root out that many wolves. Poland today has close to 40 million people.

Since the cold war, Americans have tended to believe that there was no independent state of Poland, just one more Soviet-satellite. When President Ford declared during a 1976 Presidential debate that the Soviet Union did not "dominate" Poland, he was making a legitimate point, one that in typical campaign frivolity was ignored in publicity about his "gaffe." Those who know Poland, however, know it is not a Soviet satellite. Its church, workers, intelligentsia, and, indeed, its Communist Party are Polish, not Soviet, in character.

Three times since World War II, Poles have risen up in protest against their regime, each time winning important changes. Though Communist, the regime has demonstrated in its innovativeness that it is in fact not dominated by Moscow. Polish sovereignty is "limited" in the sense that an anti-Communist revolt would ultimately be suppressed by the Soviet Union, though at incalculable cost to Moscow, which is a formidable deterrent. "Soviet intervention," wrote British historian Edward Crankshaw of the latest crisis, "would have brought the (East European) house down. The bogus fabric of the Warsaw Pact would have been in tatters."[2] Polish sovereignty is limited in the same sense the sovereignty of a good many Western nations, particularly in the Western hemisphere, is limited. It is unlikely a Marxist takeover in Mexico today would get any further than Salvador Allende got in Chile a decade ago.

The most perilous Polish revolt prior to 1980 came in October, 1956. An August workers' revolt in Poznan spread across the country and was joined by farmers fearing collectivization of private farms. The Russians were alarmed by the sudden reappearance of Wladyslaw Gomulka, the "Polish Tito," jailed with other "renegades" seven years before, during the East European purges. With Hungary in open rebellion during the fall of 1956, Khrushchev and the Kremlin feared Gomulka might take Poland out of the Warsaw Pact and follow Tito's path into open rupture. To head off the crisis Khrushchev, Molotov, Kaganovich, and Mikoyan flew to Warsaw October 19 to confront the Poles. Gomulka faced them down.

Less than twenty-four hours later the Russians were back in Moscow, and Gomulka became first secretary of the party. In his opening speech to the party congress he announced the "full independence and sovereignty of all Communist countries and parties and the rights of each nation to sovereign self-government." Indeed, he sounded like Tito.

The irony of Gomulka's return from the cold lies in how he left power fourteen years later. A second Polish uprising in 1970 (there had also been a brief flare-up in 1968), this time was directed against Gomulka. Started (like the 1980 revolt) in the shipyards of Gdansk, the 1970 uprising took forty-one lives before it was put down by Polish security forces. Gomulka in 1970 was as combative as Gomulka in 1956, only this time against the Poles pressing for change—his change. We know from his later memorandum that he actually asked Moscow in 1970 to send in tanks to keep him in

137

power. The Kremlin turned him down. In the memorandum (written after his removal as part of the traditional *mea culpa* of fallen Communists), he said: "I did not show this message (to the Kremlin) to anybody since this would have been a death sentence upon me. It was more than my nervous condition could bear."[3]

We now have witnessed yet another crisis in which it was a question of Russian intervention. It should have been clearer this time that if Russian tanks did not roll in 1956 to prevent the rehabilitation of the Polish Tito or fourteen years later when invited in following bloody fighting, it was less than certain they would roll against Lech Walesa and the sitdown strikers of the Solidarity labor movement.

The measure of our faulty analysis of Europe today is that American officials not only expected a Soviet invasion, but openly predicted one. In the final days of the Carter Administration and early ones of Reagan, high-level official predictions from the White House and State Department came with such frequency that it seemed we were inviting the Soviets to send in their tanks, legitimizing their right to invade, seeking to create a self-fulfilling prophecy.

If there is a lesson from the latest Polish crisis it is surely that Eastern Europe, like Western Europe, no longer is immune to change. The Soviet Union, like the United States, is discovering the limits of power on its allies. Moscow could have invaded Poland in 1981; indeed, it still could invade Poland, for the Soviets cannot be happy about what is taking place. Because they have not, perhaps it is time to consider constraints on Soviet power. One such constraint was suggested by historian Wolfgang Leonhard: "the fundamental need for change and reconstruction within the bloc of Eastern Europe is dramatically obvious, and the general pressure is relevant to the Soviet Union as well."[4]

The mistake in the conventional American analysis of Soviet behavior in Eastern Europe, like the mistake in our analysis of almost *all* Soviet behavior, is to believe that the only constraint on Soviet military power is other military power. In what might be called the

"Afghanistan syndrome," we feared Soviet invasion of Poland precisely because, as in Afghanistan, no comparable military force existed to stop an invasion, at least not for long. The reality, though,
if one digs below this superficial level of analysis and regards the
situation as it is seen from Eastern Europe, is that the real forces
limiting Moscow's freedom of action today are not military but
economic and political. What our analysts failed to do as they eval-
uated the Polish situation in 1980–1981 was to put themselves in
the shoes of the Russian leaders and ask—what would an occupation of Poland accomplish?

Poland was not defecting. Reduced to its simplest level, the latest Polish crisis was a crisis of meat prices. One could go so far as
to say that each Polish crisis since the war has been a meat crisis.
Poles love meat. According to official statistics, they eat twice as
much meat as the European average (East and West Europe) or
about 160 pounds per person per year.[5] Each time Polish authorities
have tampered with meat prices in an attempt to reduce the dispar-
ity between free farm prices and controlled market prices, workers
have revolted. Even a Kremlin leadership inclined to put down
Polish protests by force must ask itself what possible utility Russian
troops would have in solving a meat shortage. Had the Russians
invaded they might have had to go into Romania as well. Soon
after the Polish protests broke out, Romanian leader Ceausescu began echoing the Poles by confessing his error in neglecting agriculture and overemphasizing rapid industrialization. Romania, too,
had a meat problem.

This was not Hungary in 1956 or Czechoslovakia in 1968, with
renegade party leaderships Moscow suspected—as it had suspected
Gomulka in 1956—of wanting to defect and abandon socialism.
The Polish problem was not renegade leadership but an entire
working population protesting an economic system that was rotten.
Ultimately, the problem was political, for the Poles obviously were
protesting defects in the system. But the changes they proposed
were an attempt to reform it, not reject it. The free labor unions,
the Catholic Church, even the majority of intellectuals wanted evolution, not revolution. The real choice facing Moscow was between

allowing the Poles to pursue a path that might, one day, make communism palatable to the majority, or, by invading and crushing the workers in their plants, permanently robbing the system of any past, present, or future claim to legitimacy. That is, assuming that the system would survive an invasion.

It was not the first time since détente began Moscow had faced such a choice, though it certainly was the most dramatic. Throughout the 1970s much of Eastern Europe had liberalized economically and eased up on political constraints as well. Hungary, under Janos Kadar, embarked on what the magazine *The Economist* called a "quiet economic revolution—capitalism." Poland, under Edward Gierek, launched its "dash for growth," which was built on Western credits and rapid industrialization. Both nations increased their foreign trade with the West to over 50 percent of total trade. Romania joined the International Monetary Fund. Eastern Europe's collective Western debt reached a staggering $75 billion, of which one-third belonged to Poland. Travel to the West, both for Poles and Hungarians, became a relatively easy matter.

Not only did Moscow permit these economic deviations, it actually encouraged them. One of the direct causes of the East European turn to the West had been Moscow's 1975 decision to raise Soviet oil prices for East European Comecon countries to levels close to OPEC levels, under the so-called Bucharest price formula. That price rise increased the price of Soviet oil to Comecon countries "to an extent unknown in that organization's history,"[6] and prompted the East Europeans to turn to the West for credits to expand industry, increase exports, and pay the higher energy costs. For Poland this ultimately would prove disastrous; the error in Gierek's "dash for growth" was to emphasize modern industry—which is not Poland's economic forte—and de-emphasize Poland's export strengths, coal production, and agriculture. Under Gierek, Poland's private agriculture sector, which accounts for 75 percent of all arable land, was openly discriminated against, and productivity and exports fell.

It once was assumed economic liberalization could only be reconciled with strict party political control by setting limits on how far the liberalization could go. Richard Portes, a leading expert on Eastern European economies, has referred to an unwritten rule, according to which Moscow would permit no Comecon country's trade with the West to pass one-third of total trade.[7] If ever there was such a rule, by 1980 it had been crushed under the weight of events, political and economic. The Eastern Europeans, like everybody else in the world, were demanding progress.

TABLE 1

Eastern Europe's Trade With the West

(in millions of dollars)

	1970	1977	1979
Poland	1,932	8,963	11,208
Hungary	1,157	3,997	5,532
Romania	1,250	4,248	7,044
Bulgaria	563	1,420	2,160
Czechoslovakia	1,494	3,961	5,508
USSR	5,393	25,742	39,312
East Germany (excluding trade with West Germany)	839	2,338	4,044
TOTAL	12,628	50,669	74,808

Source: OECD, *Overall Trade By Countries, Series A,* January, 1972; *Statistics of Foreign Trade, Series A,* July, 1980

Nor was the Soviet Union itself immune to the changes (see Table 1). Moscow's trade with the West rose from 21 to 33 percent of total trade during the 1970s, a 12 percent increase, which exactly compensated its drop in trade with Comecon. It was becoming more difficult for Soviet leaders as well to deny their citizens rising standards of living. "The Soviet population," wrote Sovietologist Seweryn Bialer, "and especially the working class, has learned to anticipate a continuous if slow rise in the standard of living. Neither we nor the Soviet leaders can predict how the working class will react to a protracted stagnation of consumption levels and continued shortages of food."[8]

Russian leaders did not hide that several successive years of slow growth (see Table 2) had begun to crimp the consumer sector. They had sought partial solutions in economic reform, trade with the West, and arms negotiations that would lead to reductions in military expenditure. At the Twenty-sixth Party Congress in February, 1981, party leader Brezhnev spoke of the "heavy burden" imposed on the Soviet economy by the country's defense budget. The American failure to ratify the SALT II treaty and the Reagan defense

TABLE 2

Soviet Gross National Product

(average annual rate of growth, %)

1973	7.0
1974	4.0
1975	1.9
1976	4.6
1977	3.6
1978	3.5
1979	0.7
1980	0.5

Source: Central Intelligence Agency

budget gave Soviet planners good cause to worry about an economy already weakened by the burden of heavy defense spending.

Clearly, the Soviet Union faced economic choices starker than during the high growth years of the 1970s. It was one thing to sustain annual defense budget increases of 4 to 5 percent when growth was 7 percent, quite another when it was less than 1 percent, as it was in 1979 and 1980. In many ways the Soviet dilemma was as stark as the American: both countries faced falling growth rates, rising defense expenditure crimping growth even further, and reduced social expenditure. Equally, both superpowers faced parallel situations with their allies: with smaller defense obligations than the superpowers, Eastern and Western Europeans alike had greater economic flexibility; they were able to shift resources to meet crisis situations and concentrate more on solving problems of growth and productivity, even if, as in the Polish case, they made bad mistakes.

Russians talking about Poles, Hungarians, and Romanians began to sound like Americans talking about Germans, Dutchmen, and Frenchmen. An oddly parallel situation was developing in which the superpowers, nervous and worried about the sour turn in their own relations, became indignant that their burdens were not shared by their allies. One American correspondent told of the latest Moscow joke: What is international proletarianism? a Russian asks another. Answer: When there is no meat in Moscow and a strike breaks out in Warsaw.[9] Thus each superpower, in different ways, began to reach over the heads of its own allies and communicate directly with the other's allies. The American bluster on Poland matched the Soviet attempt to keep détente burning in Western Europe—though the superpower light was obviously flickering.

As we have seen, Atlantic interests were diverging. In the Western camp Europeans made it clear they did not like the Reagan idea of heating up a new arms race and expecting Europe to join in without protest. In an extraordinary admission, West German Defense Minister Hans Apel, told a high-level defense meeting in Munich of a "latent distaste" in Europe today for both superpowers, and the growing idea of a "Europe for the Europeans."[10] The new Reagan approach to Moscow was an attempt to weaken the Soviet economy by denying it trade and escalating the arms race; whereas the Western European approach was to make Moscow so dependent on Western trade, technology, and credits that it could not risk endangering détente—even over Poland. A poll in the West German magazine *Der Spiegel* showed that only 38 percent of the German public wanted Bonn to adopt the new Reagan hardline against the Russians; 6o percent wanted Bonn to continue on its moderate course.[11]

These are sharp differences. In general, the Western European attitude is similar to that of the Eastern Europeans: economic exchange is the father of political change. The European view, East and West, is that as the world enters a new economic era characterized by low growth, scarcity, and rising prices, it will become, by necessity, more interdependent. This view is not totally different from what we see emerging in China, where the present leaders have recognized that China can no longer indulge the hermetic stagnation of Maoism. Eastern Europe, too, will become part of the new interdependence, and it will become a riskier option for Moscow to send its tanks rolling around to crush reform. Moscow, judging from its own reforms, seems to recognize these realities. Soviet citizens, too, have rising expectations today. A CIA study recently pointed out that 25 percent of total Soviet farm output now comes from privately held farms under reform programs begun in 1976.[12] That year, 1976, it will be remembered, was the year the Polish party under Edward Gierek tried to increase meat prices by 70 percent, was greeted by a call for a spontaneous national strike, and was forced to rescind the price rise a day later.

Why would the autocratic Kremlin leaders permit such assaults on authority and order as we have seen recently in Poland and, less spectacularly, throughout Eastern Europe? The answer seems to be that they understand the inevitability of economic reform and will accept it—even encourage it—so long as the party structure is not threatened. This gives the Eastern Europeans a large margin of maneuver. Evolution is possible in the view of Polish dissident leader Jacek Kuron "up to the limits set by Soviet tanks."[13] In a sense, the Soviet Union today is in danger of being nibbled to death by its Eastern European friends, who will pursue reform courses faster than the Kremlin likes, but never quite fast enough to risk being suppressed by tanks. Some observers see in this state of affairs the "fatal loosening of the Soviet order in the East."[14] While the loosening may not be fatal, it is nonetheless a fact.

This should be seen in everybody's interest, East and West. As Briton David Watt has put it:

. . . the real object of western policy is the creation and preservation of a situation in which there is the maximum freedom (in Eastern Europe) compatible with the maintenance of the overall political status quo. The Russians for their part want something that is, in practice, not so very different . . .[15]

But it is not seen this way in the United States. President Ford may have lost the election over an idea similar to Watt's. One of his top advisors, Helmut Sonnenfeldt, earlier had created a foreign policy scandal when his views on the ''organic'' relationship between Moscow and the Eastern Europeans became known. The official American position, one we are legally obliged to celebrate each year with ''Captive Nations Week,'' is that we will not rest until not only Eastern Euopre is liberated from communism, but parts of the Soviet Union as well. ''We are left,'' says Soviet advisor Georgy Arbatov, ''with the space maybe from Moscow to Leningrad, from Smolensk to Gorky.''[16] As numerous Poles made clear during the latest crisis, American interference is the last thing they want.

The real difference between Americans and Europeans over a policy toward the Soviet Union is not over such cold war relics as ''Captive Nations Week,'' but over the value of trade and détente as a means of influencing the Communist systems. The Western European view is that improved relations are a precondition for evolution. The prevailing American view is that détente is a sham that serves to camouflage the Soviets as they continue on their devious course: buying our grain the better to switch their own resources to arms, buying our computers the better to copy them, signing arms accords the better surreptitiously to steal ahead of us in the arms race, signing bilateral accords with us the better to cover terrorism and revolution in the Third World.

There is no doubt that the current American vision of the Soviet Union is paranoid, similar to the Soviet paranoid vision of us (and practically everybody else). That the Russians in their closed and sclerotic society view the outside world with suspicion, using a controlled and monolithic press and big lie technique to manipulate public opinion, is no reason for an open, pluralistic, and democratic society to do the same. Part of the problem may stem, as George Kennan has said, from the ''inordinate influence exercised over American foreign policy by individual lobbies and other organized minorities.''[17] Part may stem as well from the fact that many of this country's most influential Soviet scholars and commentators are of Eastern European origin, and their personal experiences color their views.

The root of the problem, though, is psychological, akin to what Michel Crozier calls the "American disease," a tendency to see things in terms of good and evil, good guys and bad guys, our side and the other side. This view that all Communism is bad and therefore all anti-Communism good led us into our greatest modern tragedy in Vietnam and is threatening again. Europeans, Crozier says, see things in more complex colors. From the beginning, he writes, "Europeans have been accustomed to see evil everywhere."[18] Seeing it everywhere, there is nothing special about the Communist evil. For Americans, if Communism is *the* evil, it follows that the Soviet Union is *the* devil. "Americans see danger, revolution and terrorism everywhere," wrote *Der Spiegel*, "and behind it all are the Russians."[19] *Time* magazine is in agreement in a cover story about Secretary of State Alexander Haig: "His world view can be summed up in one phrase: the Russians are coming."[20]

The result of this Manichaean view is that we pursue a foreign policy that is self-defeating. We support the most corrupt dictatorships on the grounds they are anti-Communist, and when they inevitably are thrown off because they are corrupt, we end up dealing with governments hostile to us for having supported the dictatorships and friendly to the Russians because they did not. Our policy on Afghanistan becomes incomprehensible: a Marxist 1978 coup in Kabul is totally ignored in Washington, hardly reported in the press, and subsequently forgotten. Over a year later, the Soviets send in troops to keep the Marxists in power, and we decide the Soviet move is in reality a drive on the West's oil supply lines in the Persian Gulf (which would be an act of war). We begin a frantic search for bases in the area, making even friendly nations squirm as they come to believe the Persian Gulf will become a new focus of superpower clashes. Saudi Arabia's Crown Prince Fahd wants no part of it. He states:

The Gulf states don't need anyone to defend them. They can defend themselves if they have the necessary weapons. Manpower and technical knowledge we already have.[21]

Showing that he is no Manichaean, Fahd adds:

The threat (to the Gulf) comes from many directions, not just from the Soviet Union. In Afghanistan they have translated a threat into a deed, and are acting exactly the same as Israel in Palestine.[22]

Our simplistic view of things opens a wedge between us and the allies, whose views, perhaps because they lack the lobbies and special-interest groups Kennan referred to, are more pragmatic. Thus when the Reagan Administration determines that American involvement in El Salvador is necessary to assure the defeat of communism, they greet us with stony silence. To them it is not as clear as to United Nations Ambassador Jeane Kirkpatrick[23] that dictatorships of the right are superior to those of the left. They have had experience with both.

The Europeans are just as evasive when we talk of extending NATO activities to the Persian Gulf region. They do not rally to America's new mood, what columnist Flora Lewis calls the "extraordinary mood of jingoism in the nation, far more intense than people abroad suspect."[24] They have seen other untried American presidents come into office with their provincial theories and be sent packing four years later.

The purpose here, lest it be misunderstood, is to give examples of how simplistic analysis of complex problems poses its own problem and contributes to American isolation. It is time to correct the conventional view that all Russians are evil, all Europeans appeasers, and all Americans sheriffs drawing lines in the dust. In Europe the tendency is to be less paranoid, to focus more on the formidable weaknesses of the Soviet Union, and how to exploit them. Is it not possible that, in America, we overrate the Russians, have become so obsessed with them that we no longer focus on our own objectives, simply set objectives that are the opposite of theirs?

Despite American help, it would be difficult to demonstrate that Soviet influence is spreading in the world today or that Communism is a waxing force. As recently as two decades ago, the view of a rising Soviet tide conceivably could have been defended. On the eve of the 1960s we knew nothing of the Sino-Soviet split; we feared Communist dominoes falling around Asia, Europe, Africa, and Latin America; such key countries as Indonesia, Egypt, India, Algeria, and the Philippines were in various states of pro-Communist destablization, not to mention Guinea, Ghana, Algeria, Iraq, Mali, Sudan, Somalia, and North Yemen. "World communism" seemed on the march, and it appeared possible Communists might well construct a self-sustaining autarkic system able to remain outside the liberal systems being knitted together among industrialized nations and the developing nations.

It is a very different picture today. There is, quite simply, no "world Communist" system. Not only are the key developing countries coming to reject communism, but Communist countries themselves are rejecting it. As the Polish dissident historian Leszek Kolakowski has put it, "Communism is already in a state of slow disintegration."[25] Communist China itself may be in the process of abandoning Marxism. Those nations in the developing world that still tolerate Soviet influence—nations such as Angola, South Yemen, Mozambique, and Ethiopia—tend to be passing through post-colonial phases in which they temporarily are more comfortable with Soviet than Western aid. If the lessons of other African nations are an example, the Soviet presence there will not last long. Cuba remains unique, and it is arguable whether Cuba represents Communist success or failure. The Soviet Union, in its present state, cannot offer these developing nations the one thing they most need—markets. Moscow can provide some short-term aid, but the very nature of the Soviet system—suppression of markets and consumer needs—prevents the Russians from becoming their permanent partner—unless, of course, the Soviet economic system evolves, or the West, through a policy of short-term interest, turns its back on the needs of these countries, giving Moscow no competition.

The developing nations need the world system in which to operate—the World Bank, the IMF, GATT, the European Bank, the Export-Import Bank, the international private banking system. What's more, as we see today in Eastern Europe and the Soviet

Union, the Communists need this world system as well. As Sovietologist Robert Legvold has written, the Soviet Union "is gradually allowing itself to be drawn into an ever-increasing economic involvement with the outside world, and, indeed, consciously committing itself to a still larger one."[26]

The real question—and it is the essence of our differences with the West Europeans—is whether this interaction is in the West's interest. The Europeans, as we have seen, argue that the fruits of interdependence already can be seen in Eastern Europe and in East-West European relations. Poland is a product of détente. The prevailing American view, however, is that we are being duped by the Soviets. Here is how Samuel P. Huntington, a leading opponent of trade with Russia, describes it:

The evidence seems conclusive that [Western technological exports] have made a small, but real, impact on Soviet productivity and growth. In certain key areas, they have played a particularly significant role. It has been estimated that Soviet oil production would today be 10–15 percent less than it is, were it not for recent imports of certain types of Western technology. While the Soviets benefitted substantially from intensified economic engagement, they also continued and intensified their military buildup.[27]

The best way for dealing with the Soviet Union, holds Professor Huntington, a member of what *Foreign Policy* magazine has labeled the "anti-Soviet Brigade"[28] is not dealing with it at all—adopting policies of quarantine and containment. The idea, which is the intellectual basis for the Reagan policy of increasing the American defense budget, is to push the Russians toward economic bankruptcy and internal disruption by outspending them on defense (that we may be bankrupt and disrupt ourselves is less important). This view holds that the Soviet internal contradictions are so great that the system eventually will fall of its own weight if the West does not help prop it up. It is the newest version of Soviet apocalypse, joining some older versions.*

*The economic theory of apocalypse was first put forth by Milovan Djilas in *The New Class;* the geo-political theory by André Amalrik in *Will the Soviet Union Survive Until 1984?* the nationalistic theory most recently by Hélène Carrère

Most of these theories are intellectual exercises. The evidence suggests rather that the Soviet system sluggishly adapts to deal with its various problems. The Soviet power machine alternately presses down or eases up on controls. The policy of the anti-Soviet brigade under its various guises really is a policy of despair. Reform won't work, it holds, only revolt or war.

The record shows, however, that the Russian system, though bad, is not as bad as it was. What liberalization there has been has come in with détente and did not precede it. Few people claim the Soviet system is more repressive than it was under Stalin. The system, judged by Western standards, is odious, but then Russian systems always have been odious, judged by our standards, except perhaps under Peter. The point is how to influence it to become less odious. We already have had some influence. As Kolakowski has put it, "the Soviet leaders cannot go back to a pure form of Stalinism for fear of jeopardizing their own power and bringing the country economically even lower than it is."[29]

These differences in view are reflected within the Soviet Union itself, and we obtain some knowledge of them through the dissident movement. The Solzhenitsyn approach is the American apocalyptic approach: "Communism will never be halted by negotiations or through the machinations of détente. It can be halted only by force from without or disintegration from within."[30]

Solzhenitsyn urges the West to cut all ties with Moscow, turn on the pressure, accelerate the arms race, and let the Communist contradictions do the inevitable rest. Arms control must be avoided at all costs, for it is through Soviet arms spending and neglect of the citizen that the internal pressure will increase.

The Soviet Union's other best-known dissidents do not agree. Andre Sakharov, though having some points in common with Sol-

d'Encausse in *Decline of an Empire*. These theories all hold that the Soviet Union is condemned to disintegrate. They share points in common with the Marxist view of capitalism, also doomed, thanks to internal contradictions, to ultimate collapse. One wonders what will be left when both are gone—perhaps just Europe's "Middle Way."

zhenitsyn, is not an apocalypticist. Sakharov believes the West should relentlessly apply political and economic pressure on Moscow, but as a means of forcing the regime toward reform, not collapse. The trouble with the Sakharov approach, argues fellow dissident Roy A. Medvedev, is that it doesn't work. Direct pressure from the West, says Medvedev, either military or economic, plays into the hands of the most conservative elements in the Politburo and strengthens the regime's resistance to reform and change. Says Medvedev:

The relaxation of tensions is a necessary precondition, though not the only one, for the development of democracy in Soviet society. A country isolated and cut off from the outside world by various cold war factors becomes insensitive to protests and views beyond its borders.[31]

An illustration of this argument is provided by statistics on Soviet Jewish emigration. Emigration is possible and expands as a price the Soviets are willing to pay for improved trade with the West, a classic example of trade as a lever. Emigration, however, contracts, when direct public pressure is applied: for example, the Jackson–Vanik and Stevenson amendments to the 1974 trade bills, attempted to force quotas on the Soviets. It took six years—until 1979—for Soviet Jewish emigration to reach the pre-amendment levels of 1973 (see Table 3). In 1980, following Afghanistan and the grain embargo, it slumped back to the 1974 level.

An interesting corollary to Roy Medvedev's theory has been offered by brother Zhores Medvedev, now in exile in London.* Zhores has written of reforms instituted in Soviet agriculture as a result of the 1980 American grain embargo applied after the invasion of Afghanistan. The embargo, writes Zhores, "had an important stimulative effect, forcing the leaders to mobilize all reserves and potentials for the development of agricultural productions and to implement some new reforms. . . . Internal agricultural policy now clearly tends to be more liberal and flexible."[32]

*Zhores (the name is an homophone for Jaurès, family name of Jean Jaurès, France's great turn-of-the-century socialist leader), a soviet biologist, was incarcerated by the Soviets in an insane asylum for his dissident activities before brother Roy's protestations got him out and into exile in London.

What are we to make of this? One brother claiming trade leads to reforms, the other that trade embargoes bring reforms. The reconciliation of these two conflicting notions is found in the following idea: that the Soviet-American grain agreement of 1975 led to higher expectations by Soviet citizens, expectations the Soviet leadership must now see are met. If domestic production falls, grain must be imported; if grain imports are cut, reforms must be introduced. As the CIA paper earlier referred to pointed out, '' a primary plank of the (Soviet) consumer program has been the promise to improve diets, especially by way of expanding meat output.''[33]

TABLE 3

Emigration of Jews From the USSR

1972	31,903
1973	34,903
1974	20,695
1975	13,549
1976	14,213
1977	16,736
1978	28,864
1979	51,320
1980	20,975

Source: *Greater New York Conference on Soviet Jewry,* January, 1980

It would be somewhat more difficult to realize this meat reform program if, following invasion, the regime suddenly found itself obliged to provide Poland (and perhaps Romania) with meat as well. The Soviet Union has the power to invade Poland, but the conclusion of any objective analysis must be that it is the last thing the Russians want to do. Economic problems demand economic solutions.

Brezhnev will leave his empire in somewhat better economic and military health than he inherited it, but all is far from well. To be surrounded by hostile neighbors, afflicted by falling economic performance, and confronted by a domestic population increasingly aware of the defects of the system cannot be a comfortable feeling.

Something must be done. In the end, Lech Walesa and the Solidarity union movement may turn out to have forced changes on the sclerotic Communist system that will be the salvation of the system in Russia as well.

Notes for Chapter 9

1. Quoted in A. J. P. Taylor, *The Struggle for Mastery in Europe* (Oxford: Oxford University Press, 1971), p. 134.

2. *Observer* (London), December 7, 1980.

3. *New York Times*, January 26, 1981, p. A10.

4. Wolfgang Leonhard, "Are We Moving Toward a Post-Communist Era?" *Encounter*, November 1980, p. 23.

5. *Times* (London), February 23, 1981, p. 5.

6. Raimund Deitz, *Soviet Economy in a Time of Change,* Congress Joint Economic Committee, 1979, p. 263.

7. Richard Portes, "East, West and South: The Role of Centrally Planned Economies in the International Economy," prepared for the Harvard Institute of Economic Research, 1978.

8. Seweryn Bailer, "Poland and the Soviet Imperium," *Foreign Affairs,* Vol. 59, No. 3, p. 534.

9. David Willis, *Christian Science Monitor,* December 18, 1980, p. 1.

10. *Die Zeit,* March 6, 1981, p. 4.

11. *Der Spiegel,* February 9, 1981, p. 34.

12. Deitz, *Soviet Economy in a Time,* p. 763.

13. *Encounter,* November 1980, p. 28.

14. John Lucas, "The Light in the East," *New Republic,* September 10, 1980, p. 17.

15. David Watt, "The Atlantic Alliance Needs Leaders Who Face the Facts," *Economist,* October 11, 1980, p. 23.

16. *New York Times,* October 5, 1980, p. E3.

17. George Kennan, "Cease This Madness," *Atlantic Monthly,* January 1981, p. 25.

18. Michel Crozier, *Le Mal Americain* (Paris: Fayard Publishing Company, 1980), p. 283.

19. *Der Spiegel,* March 9, 1981, p. 20.

20. *Time,* March 16, 1981, p. 23.

21. *Der Spiegel,* March 2, 1981, p. 30.

22. *Ibid.,* p. 32.

23. Jeane Kirkpatrick, "Dictatorships and Double Standards," *Commentary,* November 1979.

24. Flora Lewis, "The Jingo Issue," *New York Times,* September 23, 1980, p. 23.

25. *Encounter,* January 1981, p. 21.

26. Robert Legvold, "The USSR and the World Economy," prepared for Council on Foreign Relations, March 1979, p. 1.

27. Samuel P. Huntington, "Trade, Technology and Leverage: Economic Diplomacy," *Foreign Policy,* Fall 1979, p. 69.

28. ———, *Foreign Policy,* Winter 1979, p. 28.

29. *Encounter,* January 1981, p. 21.

30. Alexander Solzhenitsyn, "Misconceptions About Russia Are a Threat to America," *Foreign Affairs,* Spring 1980, p. 806.

31. Roy A. Medvedev, *De La Democratie Socialiste* (Paris: Grosset, 1972); see also Medvedev, *On Soviet Dissent* (New York: Columbia University Press, 1980).

32. Zhores Medvedev, "The Grain Embargo: I," *New York Times*, February 10, 1981, p. A23.

33. Deitz, *Soviet Economy in a Time*, p. 762.

CHAPTER 10

The Defense of Europe

"No one in America can say if, where, how and to what extent American
nuclear weapons would be employed to defend Europe."[1]

GENERAL DE GAULLE, 1963

THE HISTORY OF ATLANTIC DEFENSE since de Gaulle has been a
history of Americans and Europeans trying to prove de Gaulle was
wrong. For Americans, our nuclear "umbrella" covering Europe
was sacrosanct: a Soviet attack on Western Europe would be regarded as an attack on the United States itself and ultimately dealt
with by nuclear weapons buried in American plains and hillsides
and on our aircraft and submarines permanently circling the globe.
For Americans and non-French Europeans, de Gaulle had blas-
phemed. Deterrence, to be credible, could not be questioned. The
link between the defense of Europe and American missiles across
the Atlantic—called "extended deterrence"—was sacred.

Strategic modifications were required from time to time. The
original strategy on which extended deterrence was based, called
"massive retaliation," was only good until the Soviet Union acquired its own capacity for nuclear retaliation in the 1960s. It was
one thing to threaten total annihilation of a foe when he could do
nothing about it, something else when he could do the same to you.
Under the Kennedy Administration, a new strategy called flexible
response was introduced, which Americans thought more credible.
From the American point of view, flexible response had an additional advantage: it transferred nuclear war from American to Western European soil. An observable tendency in Atlantic strategy over

the past two decades has been each partner trying to guarantee that nuclear war, if it came, came on the other's territory. Under flexible response, the Kennedy Administration inceased to 7,000 the number of tactical nuclear warheads in Western Europe.

Flexible response was, though few would admit it, proof de Gaulle was right. De Gaulle claimed no nation would use nuclear bombs against a third nation to defend a second nation if it was itself vulnerable to nuclear retaliation. By transferring tactical nuclear weapons to Europe, the United States introduced the idea of limited nuclear war—limited, in this case, to Europe. By introducing concepts such as firebreak and pause, the United States was saying that nuclear conflict need not escalate to the level at which American and Soviet territory would be touched. A strategic nuclear war, one that affected the United States itself, was to be avoided, but a tactical nuclear war, affecting Western Europe only, became more plausible.

The reasoning behind flexible response was so mischievous from the European point of view that one wonders how NATO survived at all. France, of course, did not survive as a member. De Gaulle in 1966 announced his country's withdrawal from NATO's military command and demanded that NATO leave French territory. Nuclear power, said de Gaulle, had changed the nature of warfare, making distant alliances less certain things. Nuclear power also tended to reduce differences between smaller and larger states, he said. Thus, for example, France could deter the Soviet Union through possession of the nuclear bomb: France need not have as many weapons, need not be able to destroy all of Russia. It was sufficient for France to have the power to destroy a few Russian cities—*arracher un bras* (tear off an arm) was the phrase, inflict destruction in proportion to the stakes France represented to Russia.

Other Europeans liked flexible response no better, but could do less about it. For them, the new strategy decoupled the United States from Europe. Massive retaliation, a strategy of pure deterrence based on the threat of missiles being fired from America, had given way to a strategy that looked like one for nuclear war fighting. For Americans, the 7,000 warheads might merely be tactical, but for Europeans each one represented a nuclear charge equal to those dropped on Japan. Moreover, NATO's nuclear charges would be falling on Western European, not enemy territory. The new strategy was in reality a strategy for stopping Soviet tanks with nuclear missiles fired in West Germany. A Soviet crossing of the Elbe river would be met, ultimately, by nuclear shells on Hamburg, Hannover, Goettingen, and Kassel, each city becoming a Hiroshima or Nagasaki of World War III. Though Americans insisted the tactical warheads were directly linked to American missiles in their Rocky Mountain silos, for the Europeans it was a highly dubious link.

With flexible response, West Germany found itself in a bind from which it still has found no satisfactory escape. Exposed, sharing a 500-mile frontier with East Germany, partly responsible for West Berlin tucked 100 miles inside East Germany, having renounced (in 1954) the right to manufacture nuclear weapons, vulnerable politically to the Soviet Union, West Germany lacked the French option. The West Germans had to settle for the best nuclear deterrent they could get, extended, flexible, whatever.

There was one alternative. De Gaulle, in the early 1960s, tried to win both Germans and British to his idea of a European confederation whose defense pillar would have rested on French, German, and British nuclear cooperation. His ideas were purposely vague, but they were clearly at odds with those of the Kennedy Administration which was lobbying hard to obtain French and German signatures on the nuclear nonproliferation treaty. Until late 1962 de Gaulle had hopes the other Europeans might join him. But that December, at a meeting with President Kennedy in Nassau, British Prime Minister Macmillan signed a new nuclear agreement with the United States, slamming the door on de Gaulle's offers. A month later the British were recompensed by the French with de Gaulle's veto of their candidature for the Common Market.

If nuclear cooperation with the French would have been difficult (but not impossible) for British politicians, it would have been a monumental act of faith for the Germans. German vulnerability made Bonn hostage not only to the Soviet Union, but to the United States. Helmut Schmidt would write in 1969 of these fateful decisions:

We must not delude ourselves about being able to counter-balance Soviet power without American support . . . without it, neither Berlin nor West Germany could be defended.[2]

Though the Germans were stuck, they, like the other Europeans, believed the new strategy lessened deterrence and left Europe more vulnerable. To dispel Europe's rampant discontent, which was threatening the Alliance, the Kennedy Administration came up with a plan that attempted to relink European defense with the American strategic force. Christened the Multi-Lateral Force (MLF), the plan called for nuclear warships carrying mixed European-American crews which would fire missiles onto the Soviet Union in demonstration of our intertwined fates. The MLF brought the second of the great post-war Atlantic defense crises and ended as tragically as the first plan, the European Defense Community, which had died in 1954. The Kennedy (and later Johnson) Administration believed MLF was infallible; de Gaulle, still trying to sell the Germans on a European force, ridiculed it; the Germans equivocated; the British worked quietly to sabotage it.

De Gaulle lobbied the Germans hard, creating great strain between the United States and France. The German Christian Democrats, now led by Ludwig Erhard, were split between German "Gaullists," intrigued by de Gaulle's proposal and, "Atlanticists," who believed in MLF. In June 1964 Erhard met President Johnson in Washington and agreed to work for the Bundestag's ratification of MLF by the year's end. Three weeks later, July 3, de Gaulle arrived in Bonn with proposals for German participation in the French *force de frappe*. But he was vague, and Erhard was not convinced.[3]

French pressure may not have been enough to rally the Germans to the *force de frappe,* but it was enough to turn them away from MLF. Not only did de Gaulle make it clear that German acceptance would be incompatible with the Franco-German and Common Market treaties, but he continued to hold out prospects for future "Europeanization" of the *force de frappe,* which interested Bonn. The Germans, aware that European unity following de Gaulle's veto of the British EEC entry was more fragile than ever, did not want to risk total disintegration. MLF was allowed to die a natural death.

Two decades later, with Western Europe having become a fully integrated economic community, run by the European Council, controlled by the European Parliament, and represented by a foreign policy and diplomacy frequently at odds with the United States, one can only regret that de Gaulle was not heeded. The absence of a European defense dimension has become a leading contributor to tensions between Europe and America. Many regretted the snub of the French at the time, being fully aware that the Macmillan-Kennedy decisions threatened permanently to separate Britain from Europe and drive a wedge between France and Germany. Such were the fruits of Nassau—though official American policy was to support a united Europe with Britain as a member.

For Kennedy there was one overriding concern—nuclear nonproliferation. Kennedy would not help the French because the French force would be independent; he would help the British because the British accepted our terms: Said Kennedy: ". . . by 1970, unless we are successful, there may be ten nuclear powers instead of four, and by 1975, fifteen or twenty. . . . I regard this as the greatest possible danger."[4]

So concerned was Kennedy with nuclear proliferation that he quietly dropped a program that had been gathering steam late in the Eisenhower Administration. The so-called Norstad Plan would have deployed a new generation of missiles targetted on the Soviet Union in continental Western Europe, including, for the first time, West Germany. Though these missiles would have remained under NATO (that is, American) control, Kennedy regarded it as an unnecessary proliferation risk. What's more, by targetting the Soviet Union directly from central Europe, Kennedy would have reestablished the direct link to strategic silos at home that he was trying to break.

Things could not have gone differently for West Germany in the 1960s. So long as Bonn lacked any ties of its own with the Soviet Union and East Germany, so long as the cold war continued, so long as access to West Berlin was impeded with one Berlin crisis after another (the Berlin wall went up in 1962), Bonn lacked freedom of maneuver. But if things could not have gone differently then, the decisions of the 1960s created formidable problems for the 1980s. None of the above restrictions on West Germany exists today. Knowing what we know, it is hard to escape the conclusion that had things gone de Gaulle's way, the United States and Europe would have a far more symmetrical and balanced relationship today, one that did not founder in a lack of American "respect" for Europe (George Ball's word), or in Europe's "contempt" for the United States (Richard Pipes').

This is understood in Europe today and is a principal reason why statesmen such as Hans-Dietrich Genscher, Lord Carrington, and Emilio Colombo have called for a new look at European defense cooperation. It is less understood in the United States. Washington worries instead about a Western Europe tendency toward "neutralism" (National Security Advisor Richard Allen's description) without understanding that the anchor of West European union is a formidable constraint on European neutralism. We forget sometimes that one of the original purposes of the EEC was to keep West Germany firmly enclosed in the West.

Few people twenty years ago could see in the decisions of the 1960s the seeds of contradiction for the 1980s. It was not at all certain Western Europe was destined to have a different relationship with the Soviet adversary than the United States. A few perspicacious souls—George Kennan is the best example—suspected what was coming, but not many would listen. Kennan, it will be remembered, had left the foreign service in part over the issue of Germany. Taking a larger view of history, it did not seem likely to him that the temporary European political system that emerged after World War II could endure. He strove to find solutions in the direction of what he believed would be the inevitable reconciliation of Europe.

Some day, it appeared to me, this divided Europe, dominated by the military presences of ourselves and the Russians, would have to yield to something more natural—something that did more justice to the true strengths and interests of the intermediate European peoples themselves.[5]

Kennan was one of the few who anticipated a situation where the American presence in Europe—far from ensuring peace and security—might impede the reconciliation of the Europeans. Thirty years ago he foresaw a situation which a contemporary political scientist has described as when:

The United States, rather than the Soviet Union, is placed in the position of using the Continent as a stage from which to pursue its conflict with the rival superpower.[6]

Sixteen years after de Gaulle's statement on the imperfection of American nuclear protection for Europe, Henry Kissinger made the following pronouncement:

And therefore I would say, which I might not say in office, the European allies should not keep asking us to multiply strategic assurances that we cannot possibly mean, or if we do mean, we should not want to execute because if we execute, we risk the destruction of civilization.[7]

Kissinger, in a speech delivered in Brussels September 1, 1979, violated the taboo of never repeating the Gaullian heresy of 1963. A torrent of trans-Atlantic abuse descended on him, as it had on de Gaulle, and he took the traditional escape, claiming he was misquoted, until the full text was available. By comparing Kissinger's statement with the de Gaulle statement quoted at the opening of this chapter, one sees the similarity.

Unlike de Gaulle and even Kennedy, Kissinger did not follow his reasoning to its logical conclusion. De Gaulle had reasoned that the dilemma posed by the American nuclear umbrella must lead Europe toward its own nuclear deterrent. Kennedy claimed the dilemma must lead America to start the nuclear war, if it came to that, in Europe. Kissinger, however, used his statement to plead for the deployment in Western Europe of new nuclear weapons targetted on the Soviet Union under a plan similar to the Norstad Plan rejected by Kennedy two decades earlier. The new plan, called theater nuclear forces modernization (TNF), proposed to deploy, by 1984, 572 American medium-range warheads in Western Europe, targetted on the Soviet Union.

The TNF program was fraught with contradictions. Backed officially in Washington as a means of countering the new Soviet medium-range SS-20 missiles and giving more flexibility to the nuclear umbrella, TNF would provide, in the words of one American official, " a direct link between the defense of Europe and the American strategic deterrent."[8] In defending it, Kissinger found himself approving a plan which purportedly would assure the very thing he denounced as impossible, for surely if solution A is rejected as incredible, then B, if it leads directly to A, is equally incredible.

A few people spotted the contradictions. McGeorge Bundy, who as security advisor under Kennedy had had a prime role in the fateful decisions of the 1960s, pointed out that the TNF "solution" actually was a step back toward massive retaliation. For Bundy, if American missiles started falling on Moscow, the Russians would likely be indifferent from whence they came. The notions of pause and firebreak, introduced under Kennedy to retard nuclear escalations, the automatic decoupling inherent in nuclear warfare of any kind would be undermined by the new strategy. The crisis in Atlantic relations, said Bundy, was not caused by any want of nuclear weapons, but by a lack of confidence. It is difficult, he wrote, "to see how the deployment of additional American systems in Europe would bolster that confidence."[9]

Others tended toward the Bundy view. Christoph Bertram, head of London's International Institute for Strategic Studies, complained that the strategic studies community was becoming "dominated by technological preoccupations, not conceptual ones."[10] West German Uwe Nerlich and American Gregory Treverton, respected members of the strategic studies community, echoed Bertram.[11] Even inside this closed and esoteric community, a feeling was taking root that new nuclear gadgetry was no substitute for political consensus and sound policy based on strong conventional military forces linked to the existing stategic deterrent.

If there was a European-American crisis of confidence as the 1980s got underway, the Kissinger-Bundy debate was central to the problem. One faction, represented by Kissinger, held essentially that it was a security crisis caused by the Soviet threat, one which could be partially countered through deployment of the new missiles. The TNF program, new Pershing IIs and cruise missiles directed at Moscow, would be the Mercurochrome for the self-inflicted gashes Europeans and Americans had taken to giving each other. Without TNF, wrote Kissinger, the Soviet Union could drive a wedge into the Alliance:

We are writing the script for selective blackmail in which our allies will be threatened, and we can respond with a strategy that has no military purpose, but only a population destruction purpose.[12]

The second faction, represented by Bundy, believed the central issue was above all political and that marginal changes in numbers of missiles or warheads on one side or the other was irrelevant. The value of the American deterrent for Europe, wrote Bundy, "rests not on numbers of warheads but on an engagement that poses a wholly unacceptable and innately unpredictable risk to the other side."[13] The Alliance needed no new linkages or couplings to deter. The essence of deterrence was not certainty, but uncertainty. Bundy professed his belief in what British historian Michael Howard once called Healey's theorem, which states that though it takes only 5 percent deterrence to discourage an adversary, it takes 95 percent to encourage an ally.

If Kissinger was partially right, it was for the wrong reasons. If part of the erosion of European confidence in the United States was related to nuclear weapons, it was not that we had too few of them, but that Europeans were coming to believe that was all we had. Probably nothing had undermined European confidence in the United States so much as our abandonment of the draft and refusal to ratify the SALT II agreement. It began to appear to many Europeans as if the United States no longer believed, as they did, in fighting men and arms reductions but had become hypnotized by weapons technology, substituting sophisticated and exotic weapons for men and defense budgets for arms control. For their part the Europeans continued to press strongly for arms talks. A British commentator described the difference between us as follows:

Geopolitics give the Europeans a powerful interest in arms control and tend to make them see the Warsaw Pact not as a distant adversary defined by the number of its missiles but as a complex group of partly European states with which the Continent has to be shared.[14]

And a West German:

The task of West German security policy must be to force both Washington and Moscow into arms control negotiations.[15]

Europeans and Americans alike agreed that the Soviets had created a problem with their new SS-20 missiles targeted on Western Europe, but the question was what to do about them. For the Europeans, the TNF project was a means of forcing the Soviets to negotiate limits on these weapons, just as Americans and Soviets had successfully limited strategic weapons in the SALT II treaty. With the rejection of SALT II, however, it began to look to the Europeans as if TNF might fail as well, forcing Europe into actual deployment of new missiles. As the West German magazine *Der Spiegel* pointed out, German sentiment ran strongly against actual deployment, and such sentiment was "not limited to the political left."[16]

What had begun in 1979 as an exercise in Alliance political solidarity became, under the Reagan Administration, a new bone of contention. Throughout 1981 the Europeans put pressure on Reagan to open talks with Moscow, even though it was clear Washington preferred to forget the talking and get on with the deployment. It was a demonstration of the difference in attitudes that had developed on the two sides of the Atlantic. Europeans still were bent on turning Europe into a zone of peace in a troubled world, while Americans were devising a new nuclear-war-fighting strategy. Europeans, however, were coming to believe that a European nuclear war simply was not to be. This view was put by Gregory F. Treverton, deputy director of the London-based Internatonal Institute for Strategic Studies:

Nuclear defense (of Western Europe) is simply not in the cards, and will not be. Heads of NATO states will neither use nuclear weapons early in a conflict (unless the other side fires them first), nor delegate responsibility for weapons release to anyone else (much less to field commanders), nor use nuclear weapons on NATO territory.[17]

We have here an eye-opening statement, yet who would challenge its basic premise—that no nation would order the use of nuclear weapons on its own territory. Thus do we have an explanation for European opposition to the neutron bomb, with its unique characteristic of being designed for use on allied, not enemy, territory. Treverton concludes:

If NATO moved to conventional deterrence, it would hardly turn existing security arrangements upside down. It would not even mean abandoning the doctrine of flexible response, just giving it a different definition. Responses to conventional threats would be conventional.[18]

What should United States policy be for the defense of Europe in the 1980s and beyond? The 1949 Atlantic Alliance treaty will remain in force and under it the commitment of the United States to come to the aid of Europe if attacked (and vice versa). The Alliance might even be expanded to include Spain, if that would help the new Spanish democracy thrive in a nation with still-lingering remnants of fascist nostalgia. But if the Alliance will survive, what of NATO, the integrated military command structure that serves it? A study done recently by four international foreign policy institutes concluded that "present institutions are inadequate and at times lack relevance for the 1980s."[19] Pointing out that the problems facing the Western nations are likely to come outside Europe, the study called for "new mechanisms" to deal with them. The difficulty with NATO is that it remains an American-dominated military structure with a limited sphere of action at a time when the allies have divergent views on military questions and the United States seeks not so much to dominate its allies as to incite them to widen their sphere of action.

Trying to force all Western policy through the military prism of NATO is like asking for Beethoven's Ninth Symphony from a local drum and bugle corps. It isn't made for that. So long as France remains outside, NATO divides more than unites the Europeans and impedes the kind of European defense cooperation that would put an end to the anomalous situation in which Europe does everything together but defend itself. It is the inability of the Europeans to give a defense dimension to their confederation and become an equal and credible security partner with the United States that has led, in George Ball's harsh but apt phrase, to "the unhealthy imbalance that erodes relationships of mutual respect."[20]

Western Europe has the means today to do more for itself so long as we do not perpetuate anachronistic arrangements that prevent it. The United States is cast in the curious role today of being Western Europe's protector, not from its principal adversary, as was once the case, but from its chief customer—Eastern Europe. It is a contradiction that cannot endure. Here is how one Western European commentator sees it:

After all, 250 million West Europeans have enough resources and strength to feel no inferiority complex in confronting the same number of Russians, especially given the much greater level of European economic development. Since they cannot rely forever on American protection and involvement, an alternative approach should be kept in reserve in case of emergency. The best way to check the Soviet military buildup and to show them that their military trump card, the last strategy left to them, will not end their problems is not to accentuate continually the 'number one' American rival but to create along another related center of power and decision.[21]

This is not such a radical thought. The Europeans already do far more than Americans credit them for. Indeed, leaving aside the deterrent value of American nuclear missiles, the Europeans provide most of the military manpower and equipment in Europe today. Every continental nation maintains the military draft, even ones such as Denmark or Holland that routinely pass in America for neutralist or pacifist. In the Alliance, the only nations that have not maintained conscription are the three Anglo-Saxon ones, the United States, Canada, and Britain. Of 3.1 million men under arms in Western Europe today, 2.8 are Western Europeans. If American manpower is added to this, Western strength seems overwhelming. While Western military men are fond of insisting that Soviet forces would roll through Western Europe today as the Nazis did in 1940, the facts suggest a different conclusion. As the IISS has pointed out:

. . . apart from having greater economic resources, Alliance countries, including France, maintain rather more men under arms than the Warsaw Pact. For Army-Marines the figures are: NATO, 2.8 million; Warsaw Pact, 2.6 million. And the Soviet Union has a large number of her divisions and men on the Chinese border.[22]

One must add, as West German strategist Egon Bahr does, that it is hardly fair to count Warsaw Pact countries as we do NATO countries. Whose side would Poland be on in an East-West conflict?

Not only do the West Europeans already contribute more men (the combined European NATO countries have 2.8 million men under arms, compared with a 2.1 million for the United States), but they contribute 86 percent of the aircraft in Europe and 75 percent of the tanks (and frequently superior tanks). The problem is, of course, that since the French withdrawal from the NATO military command, the European forces are not combined. It is this anomaly we should seek to remedy.

To a certain degree the security problems posed by the French withdrawal from NATO were overcome during the past decade. Since the mid-1970s, the unofficial Gaullist military doctrine known as sanctuarization has been abandoned. Under the present doctrine, France would participate in a forward defense of Europe inside West Germany and would use French nuclear weapons against the invader if necessary. In 1979 Yvon Bourges, the French defense minister, explained the doctrine as follows:

The destiny of France cannot be separated from that of the Continent. The sovereignty of France would be seriously affected by the loss of freedom of our neighbors by one manner or another. That is why one of the essential missions of French armed forces is to participate in the defense of Europe.[23]

Despite the clear evolution since de Gaulle's era, no official cooperation between French and NATO forces exists. The French maintain bilateral national ties with other European military forces, in particular those of West Germany, but the French exception continues to deny Europe the kind of formal defense dimension it needs to look after the EEC's growing political and economic interests both inside and outside Europe.

European defense cooperation would not need a collective nuclear deterrent. The Europeans have no desire to renounce the American strategic deterrent, even if they don't entirely believe in it. It is likely that the closest Europe will get to a collective nuclear deterrent is the kind being offered by France to her neighbors. The European defense dimension should, above all, come in greater cooperation among its conventional and overseas intervention units, supported by the nuclear capability of the French and British forces.

Some will ask, why seek changes in NATO today? The system has served us well for a third of a century, deterred Soviet aggression, kept the peace in Europe. In a recent edition of *Foreign Affairs* two Europeans, one French, one West German, tried to deal with that key question.

For the West German, Joseph Joffe, an editor of *Die Zeit,* the "widening gap" between Americans and Europeans today is caused by our failure to develop new institutions to deal with the new situation in Europe. For Joffe the problem is above all the new mood of cooperation and stability in Europe. Indeed, writes Joffe:

. . . Fear would have simplified the problem considerably. It would have fused the cracks and galvanized joint action; it would have dramatized security gaps and driven Europe closer into the arms of the United States, as in the 1950s.[24]

For Joffe, the problems are caused in large part by the United States forcing policy on Europe that Europe does not want. Indeed, for him Europeans and Americans have lost their former common perspective. Atlantic disputes, he writes, are fueled by "solid differences in situation and interest." On both sides of the Atlantic, "interest in the other is shrinking."[25]

The Frenchman, Pierre Lelouche, a defense specialist, is less analytical and more prescriptive. The objective today, he states, should be to "encourage a greater European contribution and responsibility in defense of the Continent," one that "accurately reflects the historical stage at which Europe now finds itself, namely halfway between a much weakened Atlantic system and a still embryonic European framework."[26]

What American would disagree with the notion that Europe should do more for its own and the West's security? Yet, as we have seen, the policies we have pursued for over a decade have tended in the opposite direction, pushing Europe toward more dependence on us and consequently less willingness to do the necessary in its own defense.

The TNF decision, as Joffe points out, is a classic illustration of this. What could possibly do more to discourage a greater European "contribution and responsibility," than an American-produced, owned, and operated missile based in Germany and targetted on Russia? Is it not inconsistent with a Continent that is developing its own policy toward Eastern Europe? Why not let the French develop a new theater missile for Europe to counter the Soviet SS-20, which, as President Mitterand says, must be countered.

A final word on TNF. It was an allied action taken in response to the Soviet SS-20. As things stand, there appears to be little hope of obtaining reductions in or elimination of the SS-20 without going ahead with TNF. Though no strategic justification for the deployment of American theater systems in Europe exists, the program should proceed in the interest of arms control. At this point, however, no satisfactory solution to TNF negotiations with the Soviets can even be envisaged. European public opinion does not want deployment of the new land-based missiles we seem to be heading for. If new missiles are to be deployed, they should be put either on submarines or confined to air-launched cruise missiles in NATO's strategic bombers.

It must be assumed Soviet diplomacy will see the inconvenience of having new American missiles targeted on the Soviet Union introduced one way or another into Western Europe two decades after the cold war technically ended. The Russians are particularly likely to see the inconvenience for them of the cruise missile buzz bombs of the type made famous by the Nazis forty years ago (improved today by the addition of range, speed, and nuclear warheads). If they see those inconveniences, they will negotiate to reduce if not eliminate the SS-20, the cause of the problem. If they do not, they will be responsible for the very thing they have striven for years to prevent, the nuclear rearmament of West Germany under, of course, the American mantle.

As for those who suggest that any kind of tampering with NATO would produce something worse than what we have, consider the case of France. France once was the maverick (if not renegade) of the Western world. Expelling NATO in 1966, France turned toward the Soviet Union and followed a path that isolated the French not only from America but from her European neighbors. From bad during the Kennedy period, Franco-American relations became terrible during the Johnson-Vietnam years. It took President Nixon's pilgrimage to Paris a month after his 1969 inauguration to set things right again.

But what do we find today? France has become the one country with which the United States has no quarrel over defense spending. Though passing for years in NATO circles as the least loyal, most anti-American of all Europeans, France now lays out more of its GNP for defense than the loyalists. Independence has its price. France, along with West Germany, maintains the most men under arms of the major European nations and also maintains and modernizes the world's third largest nuclear deterrent force. So perverse is this reality that France, once the principal problem of the Alliance, today has become the favorite child, singled out by Americans for special praise. General Bernard Rogers, commander-in-chief of NATO forces (and therefore *not* of French forces) stated recently that "France has become an example for NATO. . . . If all the allies did as much as France, we would be much stronger."[27] De Gaulle would be amused.

General Rogers is no better than most in drawing conclusions from his logic. Indeed, it seems to be totally ignored that the one *way* the Europeans *will* do more for defense is if they do it themselves. Charles Hernu, the French Socialist defense minister, made this ironic point when he stated shortly after taking office that, "France is less threatened by neutralism than the European countries integrated into NATO."[28] As things stand, the European allies, excepting France, have become experts on devising new defense schemes that cost Americans more. It becomes something of a contest to see who is most loyal to NATO, and not only the Europeans play. Mark MacGuigan, the Canadian external affairs secretary, after an early call on the Reagan Administration, came away expressing Canada's "total support" for the new Washington hard line toward Moscow. And why not? Canada, with the exception of Luxembourg, spends less of its wealth on defense than any other NATO country.

With American foreign policy still determined by men who grew up in the tumultuous years of the cold war, it is hard to admit that NATO provides the United States with few returns today. While its costs are real—inflation, bloated defense budgets, neglected domestic programs, resentful allies—we get back little. A traditional response is that NATO still provides us with hegemony over the Europeans; that our protection of them affords us influence over them. Any student of the 1970s, however, must conclude that this simply is not so. True, the Europeans are masters at nodding our way; occasional obeisance is still our due; it remains ritual in France for any new President—Gaullist, Socialist, perhaps even Communist—to pledge immediate allegiance to the Atlantic Alliance. But the fact is that the French, like the others, follow policies that suit them, not us. They negotiate with the Russians as it suits them; they deal with us as it suits them; they run their politics and economics as it suits them. American "hegemony" over Europe today is a myth. It is not enough to keep Communists out of European governments, obtain a European boycott of the Olympic Games or terminate their negotiations to build a trans-Siberian oil pipeline. It is not enough to make them spend more on their own defense.

The one thing "hegemony" does provide is a less purposeful and cohesive Europe. If that is what Americans want, we have no business complaining that Europe is not living up to its defense commitments, is going neutralist. A stronger, more defense-minded Europe can only be had at the price of some American disengagement.

This does not mean a rush back to the Mansfield Resolution of the Seventies and the halving of American troops in Europe. There is no good reason to bring American troops home so long as they are not needed elsewhere. Indeed, as the United States faces the rising evidence that we need some kind of obligatory national service to re-infuse this nation with a sense of national purpose, solidarity, and sacrifice, we are probably better off keeping some troops abroad. But an integrated military command of fourteen nations under an American commander-in-chief is not needed for this. It is perfectly reasonable in any alliance to keep troops stationed in an allied country. We could maintain bi-lateral defense links with all the European countries, of the kind France now maintains with her neighbors, without losing anything but a certain number of military bureaucrats. What the Alliance needs today is less integration and more disintegration.

Is this such a radical thought? Is Europe today the only place that can "rebel," as the title of this book suggests, that can adapt policies to new realities and break with the ways of the past? The United States has adopted a posture today that is pathetically antediluvian, where we are perpetually trying to force allies into policies and attitudes that they do not want or share, wringing our hands and accusing them of vile sins when they do not follow. It is no way to treat your friends. Let us admit for once that while having much in common, there is much that separates us. While sharing many of the same values, much of our daily business is that of competitors and rivals. Europe has been quicker to understand this than America. It should be sufficient today to know that we would stand together in a crisis as we have stood before. We need not demand eternal pledges of fidelity. The kind of meddlesome, quarrelsome, invidious relationship we have today is a recipe for divorce. We need some respect for each other's privacy.

Notes on Chapter 10

1. Charles de Gaulle, press conference January 14, 1963, quoted in *Major Addresses*, French Foreign Ministry, Paris, p. 217.

2. Helmut Schmidt, *Stratégie des Gleichgewichts*, Seewald Verlag, 1969, p. 199.

3. For the best account of the complicated, Franco-British and Franco-German talks on nuclear defense, including Harold Macmillan's unclear offer to de Gaulle at their Château des Champs meeting in mid-1962, see Wilfrid L. Kohl, *French Nuclear Diplomacy* (Princeton: Princeton University Press, 1971), especially Chapters VI and VIII.

4. *Ibid.*, p. 245.

5. George F. Kennan, *Memoirs* (Boston: Little, Brown, 1967), p. 490.

6. John van Oudenaren, "The Leninist Peace Policy and Western Europe," quoted by Uwe Nerlich in "Change in Europe: A Secular Trend?" *Daedalus*, Winter 1981, p. 96.

7. Henry Kissinger, Brussels speech reprinted in *Survival*, November 1979, p. 266.

8. Private discussion with members of the National Security Council, December 10, 1979.

9. Speech by McGeorge Bundy to the Internatonal Institute of Strategic Studies on September 8, 1979, reprinted in *Survival*, November 1979, p. 271.

10. Christoph Bertram, "Rethinking Arms Control," *Foreign Affairs*, Winter 1980–1981, p. 359.

11. See Nerlich, *Change in Europe*, p. 71; and Gregory F. Treverton, "Global Threats and Trans-Atlantic Allies," *International Security*, Fall 1980, p. 142.

12. *Survival*, November 1979, p. 267.

13. *Survival*, November 1979, p. 267.

14. Richard Davy, *Times* (London), January 20, 1981, p. 14.

15. Theo Sommer, *Die Zeit*, February 6, 1981, p. 18.

16. *Der Speigel*, March 30, 1981, p. 23.

17. Gregory F. Treverton, *International Security*, Fall 1980, p. 149.

18. *Ibid.*, p. 150.

19. *Western Security*, a report published jointly by the Council on Foreign Relations, *Institute Francais de Relations Internationales*, *Forschungs-institut der Deutschen Gesellschaft fur Auswartige Politik*, and the Royal Institute of International Affairs; New York, 1981.

20. George Ball, "Reflections on a Heavy Year," *Foreign Affairs*, Volume 59, No. 3, p. 478.

21. Michel Tatu, *Détente and the Atlantic Nations* (Chicago: Chicago Council on Foreign Relations, 1976), p. 48.

22. *The Military Balance* (London: IISS, 1980–1981), p. 111.

23. Yvon Bourges, *Le Monde*, August 29, 1979, p. 9.

24. Joseph Joffe, "European-American Relations: The Enduring Crisis," *Foreign Affairs*, Spring 1981, p. 845.

25. *Ibid.*, p. 846.

26. Pierre Lelouche, "Europe and Her Defense," *Foreign Affairs,* Spring 1981, p. 828.

27. *Le Monde,* March 25, 1981, p. 4.

28. *Le Monde,* July 11, 1981, p. 9.

Postscript

SELDOM HAS AMERICAN FOREIGN POLICY undergone such drastic convulsions as under the last two Presidents. In the postwar period, even during the wrenching years of Vietnam, foreign policy was marked above all by a continuity that indicated that although administrations might change, policy did not. The change from Eisenhower to Kennedy caused no dramatic reversals. Perhaps under Kennedy relations with the Western Europeans deteriorated somewhat, at least relations with the British and French, but we already had been having problems with those two Europeans under Eisenhower. The transition from Johnson to Nixon was not dramatic as was expected. Johnson already had lost consensus on the Vietnam war, and the peace talks with North Vietnam had opened before Johnson's term ended. It took Nixon to end the war, but we cannot be sure the Democratic candidate in 1968, Hubert Humphrey, would have ended it under substantially different conditions.

With the election of Jimmy Carter in 1976, the thirty-year-old continuity came to an end. Carter came into office knowing nothing of foreign policy, with his advisors at odds, and by the time he was defeated in 1980 his foreign policy was in shambles. It was sometime during the Carter period that the Europeans—and everybody else—began to talk of the failure of American foreign policy, its lack of coherence, cohesion, and conviction. No longer could it be said that America had a vision of the world and our role in it and a foreign policy to reflect that vision. Lord Palmerston once said that England had no permanent friends, only permanent interests. Under Jimmy Carter it became impossible to say that either our friends or our interests were permanent.

Few people, friend or foe, were sorry to see Carter go. If German Chancellor Schmidt did not oppose Carter in 1980 as he had in 1976, it was not out of affection for him or his policies. Most Europeans preferred Carter in 1980 because they feared Reagan would be Carter all over again—another novice, another provincial—the only difference being that this one would be followed by cronies from California instead of Georgia.

And so it was, and the wrench to Reagan was as great as it had been to Carter. Gears were thrown, some of them stripped anew. A new set of foreign policies was adopted or at least proclaimed. It was not enough that Reagan arrived with a new set of economic and social principles to govern us. He also arrived with a new set of principles for presenting us to the world. How could anyone talk of permanent interests when suddenly policy was reversed by 180 degrees? Dictatorships no longer were abhorred; human rights no longer defended; arms control no longer espoused. The SALT I and II treaties were denounced and renounced because a man named Edwin Meese, who a few months before was unknown to his countrymen, stated on television that they would be.

In other countries governments also come and go. Britain, Sweden, and the Benelux countries revolve between the extremes of Labor and Conservative government; Italy, France, and Germany are dominated by vastly differing parties. But even in countries with wider political spectrums, foreign policy largely is a continuous thing. It is paradoxical that in Western Europe we find both greater political diversity and greater foreign policy consensus than in the United States. In Europe the peoples seem capable of consensus not only on national issues, but on European issues as well. De Gaulle, the man of the right, blazes the trail to Moscow and is supported by the left. In Germany the Christian Democrats rally to Social Democratic Ostpolitik; in Britain, Labor comes to support the Common Market; in Italy, the Communists support the Atlantic

Alliance. Together, these nations stitch together common policies for the Middle East, southern Africa, Central America, the Soviet Union. "There is an increased effort," says Lord Carrington, "to collaborate together in the belief that perhaps the ten of us together will carry more weight than each of us would do alone."

Throughout this book we have cited European opinion of American foreign policy. A criticism might be made that we have been one-sided, that we have failed to include those Europeans who have praised or defended American foreign policy in recent years. The truth is that under Carter and Reagan such praise and defense have been hard to find. Indeed, even our best friends have found little to laud. The closest they have come is to sympathize with us and wonder what has become of the American consensus of past years. With only two political parties of any consequence, foreign policy consensus should not be too difficult a thing. Under Eisenhower we had one, and it lasted through the Kennedy years only to come apart during Vietnam. What has happened since then?

The answer is that the world has changed and so has America, and we have gone in different directions. Not long ago Stanley Hoffmann disagreed with Michel Crozier's diagnosis of *le mal Americain*. The problem was not, said Hoffmann, that we take too moral a view of the world, but too simplistic a view. We continue to try to force a complex world of multiplying power centers, regional cartels, and crumbling alliances back into a neat East-West box. Indeed, the most rabid of the new foreign policy defenders, men such as Norman Podhoretz, editor of *Commentary,* want more than just new cold war policy of containment of the Russians and call for a new policy of containment of communism, which would mean, presumably, judging each issue not by the factor of Soviet involvement, but by that of Marxist involvement. This would automatically set us against every progressive or Marxist regime in the Third World, including that of China. One can hardly conceive of a policy that would be more self-defeating and, ultimately, isolationist.

If the world has changed, so have we. George Kennan has written of the "fragmentation" of American foreign policy that made it impossible for foreign governments to know who made it. Did one talk to American Presidents, self-admitted know-nothings on foreign policy? Did one address their advisors? And if so, which, for seldom did they agree. Did one talk to Congress or the labor unions? For Middle East policy, did one talk to the American Jewish Committee? Where did one turn?

What were the causes that in the short space of two decades turned American foreign policy from consensus to fragmentation? Here was Kennan's partial list:

The susceptibility of the political establishment to the emotions and vagaries of public opinion, particularly in this day of confusing interaction between the public and commercialized mass media; the inordinate influence exercised over foreign policy by individual lobbies and other organized minorities; the extraordinary difficulty a democratic society has in taking a balanced view of any other country that has acquired the image of a military and political enemy. [1]

These points merit consideration, for something has gone wrong. It does no good to say that things are different under Reagan, that we have found a new consensus and that consensus is called neo-containment. Such a reply is false, since many who supported Reagan did so not out of sympathy for his foreign policy views, but because they had come to believe Carter was a mistake. In truth, the choice in 1980 was not a good one, but then our system has not produced many good ones lately.

One swims upstream today suggesting that the Reagan view is wrong. The mood is toward simplicity, toward an Occam's razor approach, toward a return to traditional values. The mood is to give these new policies a chance, on the grounds that nothing else has been working. But we should not confuse Carter's failure with a Reagan consensus. These are fundamental changes being introduced into our society, and they cannot be accepted by people who believe they are wrong. The extraction of government from the governing process is not in the American interest—not even in economic terms. A massive increase in military spending is not in the American interest—not even in military terms. The definition of foreign policy as "the Russians are coming" is not in the American interest—not even in terms of containment. We will build no consensus around such flimsy ideas. We may try them on the grounds they are new—as we tried Jimmy Carter for a while—but they will not outlive a single, four-year Administration. The root problem is a total lack of American homogeneity. America is not a melting pot, but a pot that wouldn't melt. No other nation is comparably diverse and distinct, except perhaps the other immigrant nations of America, and they hardly are examples. Compared with the American potpourri, all the countries of Europe are velvety fondues, melted down years ago. If there is any other country that resembles us in this respect, it is the Soviet Union, with the difference of its being a dictatorship, in which minorities are ignored and suppressed, through perhaps not forever. American heterogeneity leads us into a kind of government by standoff, where we don't really progress, just take turns blocking the rival group.

There is probably no solution to this save good or great leaders who can bring out what we have in common, but we have had none of those lately. Perhaps the system will produce no more. But in terms of this story, in terms of our foreign relations, the American system of defining foreign policy by the "primal facts of ethnicity," to borrow the phrase of Nathan Glazer and Daniel P. Moynihan, is driving us apart from our allies. It is becoming more difficult to make common policy with Europe in any of the key areas of the world, toward the Soviet Union, the Middle East, black Africa, the developing world.

What for the Europeans was a necessary evil while they gathered themselves together is now less so. Today they will make foreign policy on their own rather than be victims of, to employ the words of Maryland Senator Charles Mathias, Jr., America's "dubious political tradition of political appeals to separatism and parochialism, to the frequent neglect of the common interests and aims of all Americans." Mathias might have added, "and their allies." This is the real difference between Americans and Europeans today. It is not one that will be easily bridged.

Notes to Postscript

1. George F. Kennan, "Cease This Madness," *The Atlantic,* January 1981, p. 25.

Index

Index